No doubt you have had times in your life when your faith has been shaken. Perhaps you have cried out to God and asked, "How long will you ignore me?" We can find comfort and perspective in the book of Habakkuk where similar questions are asked and answered.

Pastor Bruce B. Miller takes us through a spiritual journey of Habakkuk in his new book, *When God Makes No Sense: A Fresh Look at Habakkuk*. He also provides a study guide based on the WISDOM Process and QR codes so you can watch relevant videos. This is a resource you need and your church needs to answer the toughest question of all: when God makes no sense.

**Kerby Anderson, President, Probe Ministries International and host of the Point of View radio talk show**

This is a book for our times, based on God's timeless message in Habakkuk. In a chaotic, terrorized world, where down seems up and up seems down, people of faith are often riddled with questions and doubts. In this intensely practical and biblical commentary, Bruce interacts with the prophet's reflective and robust faith. Each chapter calls us to resonate with Habakkuk's heartfelt questions and rest in the truth that waiting time is not wasted time because God is in control all of the time. I commend this short, readable, and impactful book, and suggest you use it for personal reflection followed by Small Group interaction based on the author's powerful "Six-Step W.I.S.D.O.M." method.

**Rowland Forman, Founder and Ambassador, Living Stones Leadership Ministries, New Zealand, Mentor-to-Pastors, and author of *The Lost Art of Lingering: Mutual Mentoring for Life Transformation***

# WHEN GOD MAKES NO SENSE

## A FRESH LOOK AT HABAKKUK

Other books and studies by **BRUCE B. MILLER**

*Big God in a Chaotic World*
*A Fresh Look at Daniel*

*Sexuality*
*Approaching Controversial Issues with*
*Grace, Truth and Hope*

❧

*Same-Sex Marriage*
*A Bold Call to the Church in Response*
*to the Supreme Court's Decision*

*Your Church in Rhythm*

*Your Life in Rhythm*
*Your Life in Rhythm Study Guide*

*The Leadership Baton*
*The Leadership Baton Group Study Guide*
(written with Rowland Forman and Jeff Jones)

BruceBMiller.com

# WHEN GOD MAKES NO SENSE

## A FRESH LOOK AT HABAKKUK

---

the WISDOM SERIES

## BRUCE B. MILLER

Dadlin Media
— wisdom for life —

McKinney, TX

Dadlin Media is the publishing ministry of Dadlin Ministries, an organization committed to helping people develop Wisdom for Life.

For more information please go to http://BruceBMiller.com.

ISBN-10: 1-68316-016-9
ISBN-13: 978-1-68316-016-8

*Printed in the United States of America*
Unless otherwise noted, all Scripture quoted by permission. All scripture quotations, unless otherwise indicated, are taken from the NET Bible® copyright ©1996-2006 by Biblical Studies Press, L.L.C.

Abbreviations for various translations:
**NIV**, *New International Version* (2011)
**ESV**, *English Standard Version*
**NET**, *New English Translation*
**NLT**, *New Living Translation*
**HCSB**, *Holman Christian Standard Bible*

McKinney, TX 75070
BruceBMiller.com

# CONTENTS

For many of us, Habakkuk is only a strange name we memorized when we learned the books of the Bible—perhaps way back in Sunday school. We may have also learned that this book is listed in the "Minor Prophets." In fact, that is my experience—until I got into serious Bible study! But even then, this small, but powerful book of the Bible was way on the "back burner" of my mind for many years— even as a professor and pastor.

However, that changed dramatically when I was asked to do the *Life Essentials Study Bible* by Broadman and Holman. There was no way I could bypass the message of this unique prophetic book—and its relevance to all of us today. To be perfectly honest, had I known what I now know, I would have used Habakkuk's openness and honesty with God to help people who are facing the same unanswered questions as this Old Testament prophet.

Thankfully, my good friend and fellow pastor, Bruce Miller, has filled the gap for all of us. Here's a small but very impactful book that mirrors Habakkuk's brevity but at the same time helps all of us learn and apply the enduring truths that emerge from the Old Testament!

To whet your appetite, do you have questions about life's realities that are still unanswered? Welcome to the world of Habakkuk! Furthermore, what if these questions are never answered—at least on this side of eternity? Again, welcome to the world of Habakkuk! Perhaps the greatest truth that emerges from this Old Testament prophet—and which is quoted three times in the New Testament—is embedded in these life-changing words: "The righteous shall live by faith" (Habakkuk 2:4).

This biblical study is unique. Not only do you have an expositional overview, but

Bruce follows through with the "WISDOM Process"—an approach to studying Scripture that is simple—but yet profound! It's life changing!

> Dr. Gene A. Getz
> Professor, Pastor, Author
> www.bibleprinciples.org

# ACKNOWLEDGMENTS

A first-time guest asked if I had been told in advance that he was coming to church and if I knew about him because he felt the message was specifically directed toward him. Of course, I had not known about him. God was at work as only he can do, taking his Word by the power of the Spirit and using it to change hearts. Week after week, people told me the series on Habakkuk spoke directly to them and was just what they needed to hear.

Several people encouraged me to turn these messages into a book, and now you have it. One of those was Iva Morelli who has encouraged me to write and has used her gifts to edit this book with her skillful hand.

I thank God for my fellow elders and pastors who together lead Christ Fellowship to become people helping people find and follow Christ. It is a joy to serve the people of our church who responded so strongly to the sermons on which this book is based.

Our friends, Dean and Shelley Frew, graciously provided their cabin in Red River,

New Mexico for my wife, Tamara, and I to take a week of rest. There in the mountains, I prayerfully first recast the manuscripts into the book you are reading. I thank God for Tamara who prays for me daily and stands by me in the storms and blessings of life.

On our vacation, we hiked into the mountains where we saw numerous deer hoof prints in the snow. No matter what happens, arm in arm we rejoice because of the Lord. He is our strength who enables us, like the deer, to negotiate the rugged terrains of life (Habakkuk 3:19).

# INTRODUCTION

Planet Earth may look wonderful from a satellite, but for those who live on this dusty sphere, things can look rather grim. Rising terrorism, global tensions, economic trauma, increasing pollution, flagrant immorality, dishonesty and injustice cast a dark shadow over us earthlings. The world looks more and more like some ominous time bomb with a short fuse ready to explode.

It is little wonder that people begin to ask questions. Why is there so much hatred and hostility? Why all the injustice? Why do good people suffer? Why doesn't God do something? Why doesn't God clean up this mess? Why do people openly violate God's law and distort justice on every level without fear of divine intervention? Why? Why? Why? It makes you want to Skype God and ask him some very direct questions about his plans for this world, because from a human perspective, the current one is not making sense.

These penetrating questions are hardly new. Centuries before Christ came to this planet, an ancient prophet looked around at the violence and wickedness and cried out to God, "Why do you make me look at injustice? Why do you tolerate wrongdoing? . . . Why are you silent while the wicked swallow up those more righteous than themselves?" (Habakkuk 1:3a, 13b, NIV). Habakkuk was saying, "According to what I know of you, God, this doesn't make sense!"

Unlike other prophets who declared God's message to the people, this prophet dialogued with God about the people. Most Old Testament prophets proclaimed divine judgment, but Habakkuk pleaded for divine judgment. This little book records a fascinating interchange between a perplexed prophet and his Maker. He not only asked the mysterious "whys" that plague human-kind, he received an answer!

As we journey with Habakkuk, we too can move from confusion to confidence, from frustrated questions to faith-filled declarations. He teaches us to live by faith in a world of trouble. When life is shaking us like a leaf in the storm, we learn how to hold on to the unshakeable God who controls the storm. Prepare to encounter the God who exceeds our highest thoughts.

# HOW TO BENEFIT FROM THIS BOOK

This book provides you with four chapters on Habakkuk that can be read by themselves and a study guide that enables you to gain more insights from Habakkuk.

I encourage you to use the Study Guide to enable you to mature further with Christ. The Study Guide will direct you to read each chapter as you do the study.

The Bible is food for our souls. When we approach it prayerfully, the Spirit of God transforms our minds and blesses us with divine insights. More than anything else you could do, immersing yourself in the Word of God will grow you spiritually through the work of the Holy Spirit.

When we get alone to engage with God and focus our attention on understanding his Word, he speaks to us. But that doesn't mean we don't grow best in community. Connecting in a group to discuss what you are learning will help you grow even more. Invite a friend to do the study with you. Join a group, or start one of your own, and prepare for what God has in store!

 The WISDOM Process©

As children of God living in a hostile world, we need to learn how to think like Christ with biblical, spiritual wisdom for life.

Tested by thousands of people and hundreds of groups, the six-step WISDOM Process© offers a surprisingly simple and profoundly powerful way to think. Today we are drowning in data and starving for wisdom. We Google for information on any topic, but we cannot find wisdom for life's complex challenges. This simple process can guide you to wisdom.

You will find that you can use The WISDOM Process© not only in this Bible study but also for issues you face in ordinary life.

This process of thinking helps us move from knowing facts to transforming our lives in God's power. Most adults learn differently than children. Research into adult learning and studies of ancient education both show that people learn best when they have a reason to learn: a question to answer, a problem to solve or a mystery to unravel. All of us have these in our lives.

## ✝ Pray

### Role of Prayer

We access the guidance of God's Spirit through prayer and the Word of God. While God wants us to use our minds to study his Word to gain his revealed life direction, the Bible tells us:

> *If any of you lacks wisdom, he should ask God, who gives generously to all without finding fault, and it will be given to him.*
> —James 1:5, NIV

Bible study should be covered with prayer. Paul prayed like this for the Colossians:

> *For this reason, since the day we heard about you, we have not stopped praying for you and*

> *asking God to fill you with the knowledge of his will through all spiritual wisdom and understanding.*
>
> —Colossians 1:9

In answer to your prayers, the Spirit will shape your desires and then you will develop the mind of Christ. Rather than prayer being a specific step in The WISDOM Process© it should be threaded throughout the process of your study from start to end.

You will find that as you pray, the Spirit of God will guide you to truth. As a group, if you will prayerfully listen to the Spirit, he will direct your conversation to deep spiritual wisdom, conviction and motivation to honor God in daily life choices.

## W Work the issue: *What's really at stake?*

Prepare your heart and mind before engaging God's Word. Take a moment to pray about questions in your life and issues arising from the Scripture you are studying. Consider how the Lord may want to impact you at this time.

Bring your questions to your study of God's Word.

## I Investigate Scripture: *What does God say?*

God's Word is our authority for life. It is our guide for belief and behavior. Our lives must be grounded in the Word of God. It is our primary source of absolute, divine truth. Spend time prayerfully and carefully considering what the biblical text is saying.

## S Seek counsel: *What do wise people say?*

After studying the Scripture for ourselves, it is wise to seek the counsel of others. In Proverbs, Solomon said there is wisdom in a multitude of counselors. Wise people listen to advice (Proverbs 12:15; 13:10; 19:20). We provide you with well-researched input in these chapters to help you understand God's Word better, but of course this counsel itself must be evaluated against the Word of God.

## D Develop your response: *What do I think?*

We learn best when we actively engage. Writing down answers to questions will deepen your interaction with God's Word. Some questions are designed to increase your focus and understanding of the Scripture; others help you extend your thinking in applying God's Word to your life.

## O Openly discuss: *What do we think?*

Life transformation is increased when we sharpen each other in dynamic discussion. You will grow more if you study with a group where you can wrestle together with how to understand and obey God's Word. Together, prepared people led by the Holy Spirit will generate a dynamic in which ideas and wisdom multiply beyond what any individual could produce.

# M Move to action: *What will I do?*

Christ calls us to obey all he commands (Matthew 28:20). The point of Bible study is not simply knowledge, but obedience. We are studying God's Word to be more and more conformed to the image of Jesus Christ, to grow to maturity. The Bible tells us that hearing the Word without acting on it is like building a house on sand, while acting on the truth is like building a house on rock (Matthew 7:24–27; James 1:22–25). We are in the business of building houses on the Rock! Our study should lead us to move to action in the Spirit's power.

To understand any book that is historical, it is helpful to understand the context in which it was written. The following briefly surveys these issues.

Because of his own reputation and his promises to David, in spite of the nation's sin, God gave Judah additional time (2 Kings 19:34, 20:6) by striking against an Assyrian army besieging Jerusalem (2 Kings 19:35) in 701 BC. But God warned King Hezekiah of Judah that this reprieve would eventually end with the temple treasures and many people being carried away to Babylon, a new power that would rise in the east (2 Kings 20:17–18). This word was later fulfilled in the deportation that took Daniel and the temple treasures to Babylon (Daniel 1:1–2).

However, in 612 BC, before Daniel's birth, there was great internal dissension among the Assyrians, and their capital, Nineveh, was overrun by the Babylonians. The remaining Assyrians fled west and eventually called for help against the Babylonian expansion from their new ally Egypt.

Tossed like a leaf in the wind, Judah wavered between relying on God or, more frequently, on fading Assyria or historically dominant Egypt, the ancient regional power. When Pharaoh Necho came up from Egypt to aid the Assyrians at the Euphrates River, King Josiah of Judah blocked him at Megiddo and was killed (2 Kings 23:29). Pharaoh chose his own king for Judah, renamed him Jehoiakim, imposed tribute on Judah (2 Kings 23:34) and then continued northward.

However, on the Euphrates River at Carchemish, Pharaoh Necho and his Assyrian allies were crushed by Crown Prince Nebuchadnezzar of Babylon (May–June of 605 BC). Nebuchadnezzar quickly rushed south toward Jerusalem to deal with the puppet King Jehoiakim of Judah in Jerusalem, the home of a prophet named Habakkuk.

# 1

# WHY, GOD?!

Very few people name their sons after this prophet. His name sounds rather odd to our ears today: Habakkuk. How many Habakkuk's do you know? If you are pregnant with a boy and are looking for a unique name, you have it!

How do you even pronounce it? *Ha–Bak–Kuk.* Our goal is to learn how to pronounce and spell Habakkuk. Seriously, we have our sights set a bit higher than that, but it's not a bad starting point.

Who is Habakkuk? We know very little about him. He prophesied in the seventh century BC when God's people were in a mess. We don't know anything about Habakkuk's family or what town he was from. In fact, the book is not about him at all, but about his God, our God. Habakkuk teaches us that the more you know God, the better you are able to deal with life in this difficult world, and God is always bigger than our little minds will ever be able to contain—and that's a good thing.

Let's put ourselves back in the world during Habakkuk's lifetime. Israel and Judah had split into two separate nations. Israel had already been destroyed by Assyria. Judah remained, but had been going downhill fast under a series of godless kings. They were degenerating even further into immorality, injustice and idolatry. They were turning away from the true God. Sound familiar?

Assyria and Egypt had been the world powers, but the balance of power was rapidly shifting with the rise of Babylon who destroyed the Assyrian capital of Nineveh in 612 BC and then wiped out Egypt in the famous battle of

Carchemish in 605 BC. They were coming after little Judah. Habakkuk prophesied during a time of violent political upheaval; think Arab Spring, Syria and Somalia.

In this chaotic time, Habakkuk's little book describes an intensely personal struggle with God. The way things were happening in the world did not seem to match with a God who is supposed to be good, strong and just. Habakkuk's theology did not fit his experience of what God was doing and, more importantly, seemingly *not* doing.

Most of us come to a time in our lives when we seriously doubt or question God. You may be in a situation right now where God does not make sense to you. You are frustrated, angry, doubting, confused, and even fearful, asking what in the world is going on? Where is God when the little baby is dying of cancer— when mom is on life support with zero quality of life but keeps hanging on? Where is God when a woman is being raped? A UN report on the violence in Syria reports torture, even of children, as well as sexual violence. What is going on? Where is God?

Imagine that you are walking down the street and you see an elderly woman being attacked by a gang of thugs. Then you notice a policeman sitting on a park bench nearby. You shout to the policeman, pointing to the woman in distress. The policeman refuses to lift a finger to come to her aid and goes right on playing on his smart phone. Wouldn't you be angry with the policeman? While this is not an accurate picture of the reality with God, this is how Habakkuk felt. He fumed with anger because God appeared to be doing nothing about the injustice, and that was his job! That's the essence of the prophet's protest: "God, don't you care? If you are a just God, why is there no justice?" Habakkuk stands in a long line of godly people who dared to question God: Job, Moses, Solomon, Jeremiah and Jonah. Like Job, Habakkuk shouted out at God's silence.

We ask similar questions today: Where is God in a world drowning in violence, selfishness and sin? Prepare yourself. While Habakkuk will reveal truth about God, it may not be what you thought or hoped. God himself says that we will be shocked by his answer. His ways are incomprehensible, as shocking as human blood dripping from a wooden cross. And yet, if we can grasp a bit more of who God is and how he works, we will find fresh confidence in the chaos.

Habakkuk is a unified whole with the hopeful, powerful conclusion coming in the last verses. It divides into four sections that form the basis for the four chapters in this book, but each section does not stand alone. You need to see the whole. Here's a chart of the whole book.

## HABAKKUK

| Chapter 1a | Chapter 1b | Chapter 2 | Chapter 3 |
|------------|------------|-----------|-----------|
| 1:1–11 | 1:12–2:5 | 2:6–20 | 3:1–19 |
| Watch | Wait | Warn | Worship |
| Questions | Faith | Five woes | Praise song |

The first two sections, roughly the first two chapters, record Habakkuk's dialogue with God in which he asked two sets of difficult questions. Most of the third section in chapter 2 warns the nations with five woes from God. Finally, chapter 3 ends with a praise song, a prayer of worship to our great God.

Habakkuk began with the ever-persistent question, "Why?" and ends with the everlasting, "Who?" We will see that when things are shaking, we need to trust in the One who is unshakeable. When life is shaking us like a leaf in a powerful storm, we can hold on with confidence to the unshakeable God who controls the storm.

## HABAKKUK 1:1—11

*The following is the message which God revealed to*
  *Habakkuk the prophet:*

*² How long, Lord, must I cry for help?*
*But you do not listen!*
*I call out to you, "Violence!"*
*But you do not intervene!*
*³ Why do you force me to witness injustice?*
*Why do you put up with wrongdoing?*
*Destruction and violence confront me;*
*conflict is present and one must endure strife.*
*⁴ For this reason the law lacks power,*
*and justice is never carried out.*
*Indeed, the wicked intimidate the innocent.*
*For this reason justice is perverted.*

*⁵ "Look at the nations and pay attention!*
*You will be shocked and amazed!*

*For I will do something in your lifetime*
*that you will not believe even though you*
*are forewarned.*
*6 Look, I am about to empower the*
*Babylonians,*
*that ruthless and greedy nation.*
*They sweep across the surface of the*
*earth,*
*seizing dwelling places that do not*
*belong to them.*
*7 They are frightening and terrifying;*
*they decide for themselves what is right.*
*8 Their horses are faster than leopards*
*and more alert than wolves in the desert.*
*Their horses gallop,*
*their horses come a great distance;*
*like a vulture they swoop down quickly to*
*devour their prey.*
*9 All of them intend to do violence;*
*every face is determined.*
*They take prisoners as easily as one*
*scoops up sand.*
*10 They mock kings*
*and laugh at rulers.*
*They laugh at every fortified city;*
*they build siege ramps and capture them.*

*11 They sweep by like the wind and pass
on.
But the one who considers himself a god
will be held guilty."*

Through the book of Habakkuk, we
discover complaint transformed into confidence. Mature faith humbly trusts in the God
who we can never fully understand. In the face
of evil and injustice, we wait and trust in the
wrathful and merciful Lord God who judges
evil and will fill the earth with his glory. Our
encounter with God in Habakkuk can turn our
doubts into devotion and melt our confusion
into confidence. The book begins with an
interrogation of God and ends with praise of
God. Worry is transformed into worship. Fear
turns to faith. Terror becomes trust. Anguish
melts into adoration.[1]

Habakkuk is a great book for all of us
living during the in-between time, the time
between Christ's cross and his return. In this
confusing time where evil still runs rampant
and terrible suffering happens to good people
we love, we can look to God for hope. It's OK to
ask God hard questions along with Habakkuk
as we grope through pain to understand what

in the world is going on. But be prepared, the light of insight is blinding as God supersedes our highest thoughts and refuses to be kept in our neat theological boxes.

Habakkuk's message both challenges us to repent in view of God's judgment and consoles us with his promise of salvation. The entire book of Habakkuk is only 56 verses so I encourage you to read it several times as you read this book. Pray for God to show you more of himself in the prophet Habakkuk.

In the first section, Habakkuk 1:1–11, Habakkuk asked two big questions out of personal agony, followed by God's astounding answer. Let's start with Habakkuk's questions.

## HABAKKUK'S POINTED QUESTIONS

Apparently Habakkuk had been crying out to God for a long time because his first question was, "How long?!"

## 1. "How Long?"

He demanded some response from God. In the face of God's silence, Habakkuk refused to be silent. The Hebrew word for "cry" means "to shout" or "to roar."[2] Habakkuk was upset. I've felt this way, haven't you? Sometimes we hesitate to get mad at God, but God never condemns his children who call out to him in confusion. There is a difference between cynical questions arising out of rebellion against God and honest questions from bold believers who can't see how a good God can keep letting evil run wild.

## 2. "Why?"

Why was God putting up with so much injustice and wrongdoing? Why didn't he do something about it? Obviously, he could. Did God not see it? Habakkuk had been praying, but God was not answering. I have been there. It's a terrible feeling.

Who was Habakkuk calling violent? Who was perverting justice? He was talking about his own people. Judah was torn apart by sin.

Habakkuk used six different terms to describe the situation: violence, injustice, wrongdoing, destruction, conflict and strife. These led to two huge problems in Habakkuk's mind:

- The law lacks power
- Justice is never carried out

So the wicked intimidate the innocent. Another translation says that justice is paralyzed. His whole society was full of crime, violence, corruption, unfair lawsuits and conflicts.

Habakkuk held God responsible. He felt that God was not listening. He was not intervening. He was supposed to be righteous, but he was putting up with wrongdoing and allowing justice to be perverted. This is not the God he knew. He thought God was just and powerful and would respond to the prayers of his people, but instead it appeared God was doing nothing to stop terrible evil and he was not answering Habakkuk's passionate cries for help. As we will see, the living, incomparable God will not be contained by any human being.

But notice that God never told Habakkuk he was wrong to ask these questions. It's OK to ask hard, awkward, challenging questions. Life is confusing. Jacob wrestled with God (Genesis 32). Jonah complained to God (Jonah 4). Jesus himself lamented faithfully to the Father from the cross, using the words of Psalm 22:1a, "My God, my God, why have you forsaken me?" (Matthew 27:46b, NIV).

What big questions do you have for God? Do not hesitate to ask him. In fact, if it is helpful to you, I invite you to write them down. Write the hardest questions you have for God. What really bugs you that God is doing or not doing? Consider where you are now with your questions and with God. At the end of the book, see if you have made progress as you cry out to God along with Habakkuk, and get to know God and his ways a bit better.

If the situation Habakkuk described in these first four verses is bad, God's answer seems worse.

## God's Shocking Answer

At first glance, it may appear that God's answer was not related to Habakkuk's question. In Hebrew, you can see irony here: Habakkuk insisted God "look at [this] injustice" (NIV), accusing God of not looking. God replied using the same Hebrew verb: "Look" at the nations and "look" at what I am about to do. God's response widened Habakkuk's view from local problems in Judah to international matters among the nations of the world. He opened Habakkuk's mind to see a larger and more complex set of relationships.

We learn that when God at times seems silent, that does not mean he is unaware or unconcerned. He is simply patient and has his own timelines. He prepared Habakkuk by saying, "Watch and be utterly amazed."

## Watch and be amazed

Look back at verse 5. God said, "Look . . . pay attention! You will be shocked and amazed! . . . I will do something . . . you will not believe." God exceeds our understanding, our time horizons and our ability to factor complex variables. Who are we to think that we would understand if God told us what he is doing and why?

As a parent, have you ever tried to explain what you were doing and why to your two-year-old? Did he or she say, "Sure, Mom, that makes great sense. Thanks"? No. They do not understand why they can't eat the whole cake or play with the knife or chase a ball across the street. They scream at you for being mean.

Consider that the gap between you as a 30-something parent and your two-year-old is small compared to the gap between you and the incomparable God of all. Even if he explained himself to us, we would not get it, which is good because we do not want a god who fits inside our little minds.

The Hebrew word for "shocked and amazed" includes an element of fear. God outstrips our human imaginations and scares us a bit. These verbs "to look" and "be amazed" are all plural. So God is replying not only to Habakkuk, but to all the people and even to the following generations of people, including us.

There is something stark in the tone of God's answer that makes it even more shocking. In response to Habakkuk's cry, "How long?" God said he was about to empower the Babylonians to come smash Judah. God did not dispute Habakkuk's analysis of the violence and injustice or the need to deal with it. Starting in verse 6, he simply said that ruthless destroyers are coming to smash you.

## Ruthless destroyers

We want God to deal with evil in our world and to stop pain and suffering, but we rarely think through what that means. When I hear people yell out, "G.D.," I sometimes ask if they really want him to damn someone or something, because he can and he will one day. In fact, God warned his people through Moses—all the way back in Deuteronomy 28, about 1,000 years before Habakkuk—that if they turned away from him and from obedience then,

> *The LORD will raise up a*
> *distant nation against you, one*
> *from the other side of the earth as*
> *the eagle flies, a nation whose*
> *language you will not understand,*
> *a nation of stern appearance that*
> *will have no regard for the elderly*
> *or pity for the young. They will*
> *devour the offspring of your*

> *livestock and the produce of your*
> *soil until you are destroyed.*
> —Deuteronomy 28:49–51a

This warning was about to happen. It is shocking that God was raising up a ruthless, violent people to destroy his own people for their persistent sin, but he was about to do just that.

One day, God will judge the whole world. God is the just judge of all and he will deal with evil. He will set everything right, but it will not be pretty. We need to appropriately fear God much more than we do.

In verses 6–11, God characterizes the Babylonians with about 20 details of how terrifying they were. There is no sugarcoated reality here. Imagine if this message applied to us. While America is not Israel (God's chosen people), so this text does not directly apply to the United States, still America is an unjust nation that is sinking further and further into violence and sin. The law is twisted and justice is perverted.

What if God raised up a cruel nation to conquer us? Think of the worst in history, such as Attila the Hun or Hitler and the Third Reich.

Today, imagine if God said, "Be amazed and shocked because I am empowering a group of ruthless and greedy terrorists to destroy you. They will sweep across the earth and seize what does not belong to them. They will frighten and terrify you, deciding for themselves what is right. They will come fast and alert like wolves, descending on you like vultures devouring their prey. All of them are intent on violence and will take prisoners like scoops of sand. They will laugh at your president, governors and mayors. They will capture and destroy every major city in your country."

How would you respond to God? We would certainly be shocked, astounded, and find such an act by God incomprehensible. As bad as we are, we are pretty sure that we are better than they are. As we will see in the next chapter, Habakkuk was not happy with God at all. He did not like this answer.

God was not confused about how terrible the Babylonians were. In graphic terms, he described their savage violence. They were dreadful, fearsome, merciless and cruel. They saw themselves as gods. Their military power was their god. They were like "Nietzsche's

*Übermensch* . . . Goethe's *Prometheus* and W.W. Henley's *Invictus.*"[3] They worshipped themselves. In the last line of verse 1:11, we find the stinging twist: they would be held guilty.

## Guilty

These totally self-confident, arrogant, powerful people would be held accountable to a higher power. Success digs its own grave. Think about our own lives. One focus of this passage is to call people to repent.

Let's not stand apart from the people of Judah or even the Babylonians, looking down on them from a self-righteous perch as if we weren't guilty of similar sin. Consider the sins of Judah: violence, injustice, wrongdoing, conflict, strife, abusing the law, distorting justice. Who of us has not been guilty of these in one way or another? What about the sins of the Babylonians? Evaluate yourself: ruthless, greedy, seizing what does not belong to you, deciding for yourself what is right, violent, mocking authorities, abusing others, being frightening to others. Once again, who among us has not been guilty of one of these in some way—even in your own family? Where do you need to repent?

God said they would be held guilty. They bear the weight of their sins that demands divine punishment. Here's where the gospel comes in, but you have to read more of Habakkuk to see it. In the next chapter, we will see that God's mercy and our faith are the keys. God is willing to go to dire lengths to save humanity from self-destruction. "Jesus' suffering on the cross is his ultimate appeal to a world bent on violence. God will stop at nothing in order to draw us near to himself."[4] As we see in the symbol of baptism, God washes us white as snow in the cleansing blood of his Son Jesus Christ (1 John 1:7). Jesus took our guilt on himself so that God could forgive us.

But after you trust in Jesus Christ, it is common to experience dark times of questioning when God seems to be silent. Honest questions are a healthy part of our relationship with God. In horrible times, we cry out to God. He is listening. His answers may not be what you were hoping for, but you don't have the whole picture, not even close. You don't rule the world and neither do I. With a moment's thought, we realize it would be a really bad idea if we tried to run the world. Let's leave that to God. The ultimate answer to our cry of, "Why?" is the everlasting "Who?" We will see that when things are shaking, we need to trust in the One who is unshakeable.

In his excellent commentary on Habakkuk, Bruckner asks, "Why does God give us a book with the death of Habakkuk's community as the basic plot?"[5] The Bible gives us a glimpse of reality. Death is a certainty. God is not primarily committed to our peace, security or prosperity on this earth. He is interested in our faithfulness to him in a world of pain and suffering where evil still runs wild. A major point of this passage is that we can freely ask God hard questions as we watch for God's astounding answer on a much larger canvas. In your confusion over God's apparent failure to deal with injustice, watch in utter amazement at what God will do. It may totally surprise you.

Following is the famous end of Habakkuk, which we will use as a close to each chapter:

> *When the fig tree does not bud,*
> *and there are no grapes on the vines;*
> *when the olive trees do not produce,*

*and the fields yield no crops;*
*when the sheep disappear from the pen,*
*and there are no cattle in the stalls,*
*18I will rejoice because of the LORD;*
*I will be happy because of the God who*
*delivers me!*
*19The sovereign LORD is my source of*
*strength.*
*He gives me the agility of a deer;*
*he enables me to negotiate the rugged*
*terrain.*

—Habakkuk 3:17–19

As our passage in chapter 1 ends, Habakkuk was not happy. He had more questions for God. He saw God's cure as worse than his people's sickness.

# 2

# HOW COULD YOU, GOD?

## HABAKKUK 1:12–2:5

Have you ever had your faith in God shaken? Most of us have. At my request, a few people in our church sent me some of their hardest questions for God. They touched me deeply. I will share some of them anonymously.

Have you ever prayed about something only to find it worse the next day? What do you do when God responds to your prayer in a way that doesn't make sense or confuses you? You want to scream, "No, God, you are not supposed to work that way!" Habakkuk is helping us see how to hold on to the unshakeable God when he makes no sense.

Habakkuk teaches us that the more we know God, the better we are able to deal with life in this difficult world. But God is always bigger than our little minds will ever be able to contain, so we will never fully understand him. As I mentioned in the first chapter, the book is a unified whole with the hopeful, powerful conclusion coming in the last verses. It divides into four sections.

## HABAKKUK

| Chapter 1a | Chapter 1b | Chapter 2 | Chapter 3 |
|------------|------------|-----------|-----------|
| 1:1–11 | 1:12–2:5 | 2:6–20 | 3:1–19 |
| Watch | Wait | Warn | Worship |
| Questions | Faith | Five woes | Praise song |

## HABAKKUK 1:12–2:5

*Lord, you have been active from ancient times;*

*my sovereign God, you are immortal.*
*Lord, you have made them your*
*instrument of judgment.*
*Protector, you have appointed them as*
*your instrument of punishment.*
*13You are too just to tolerate evil;*
*you are unable to condone wrongdoing.*
*So why do you put up with such*
*treacherous people?*
*Why do you say nothing when the wicked*
*devour those more righteous than they*
*are?*
*14You made people like fish in the sea,*
*like animals in the sea that have no ruler.*
*15The Babylonian tyrant pulls them all up*
*with a fishhook;*
*he hauls them in with his throw net.*
*When he catches them in his dragnet,*
*he is very happy.*
*16Because of his success he offers*
*sacrifices to his throw net*
*and burns incense to his dragnet;*
*for because of them he has plenty of food,*
*and more than enough to eat.*
*17Will he then continue to fill and empty*
*his throw net?*

Will he always destroy nations and spare
none?
2 I will stand at my watch post;
I will remain stationed on the city wall.
I will keep watching, so I can see what he
says to me
and can know how I should answer
when he counters my argument.


²The Lord responded:
"Write down this message! Record it
legibly on tablets,
so the one who announces it may read it
easily.
³For the message is a witness to what is
decreed;
it gives reliable testimony about how
matters will turn out.
Even if the message is not fulfilled right
away, wait patiently;
for it will certainly come to pass—it will
not arrive late.
⁴Look, the one whose desires are not
upright will faint from exhaustion,
but the person of integrity will live
because of his faithfulness.

*5Indeed, wine will betray the proud, restless man!*
*His appetite is as big as Sheol's;*
*like death, he is never satisfied.*
*He gathers all the nations;*
*he seizes all peoples.*

Habakkuk began with the ever-persistent question, "Why?" and ended with the ever-lasting, "Who?" We will see that when things are shaking, we need to trust in the One who is unshakeable. Mature faith humbly trusts in the God who we can never fully understand. In the face of evil and suffering, we trust in the Lord God who will one day fill the earth with his glory.

In the first chapter, we saw our perplexed prophet cry out to God in frustration. Habakkuk could not understand why in the world God was allowing violence and injustice to keep happening right in front of him. Did he not see what was going on? Did he not care? And why was he not answering Habakkuk's prayer? Habakkuk was so frustrated that he was hearing nothing from God.

Then as we saw, God answered Habakkuk, but not in the way he had hoped. God's solution made Habakkuk even more frustrated, confused and angry. God said he was going to bring the ruthless Babylonians to crush the people of Judah who had turned away from him. This made no sense to Habakkuk. It would be like God raising up Hitler to judge America. Sure we have our problems, but Hitler was worse. In Habakkuk's view, God had not solved the problem, but made it worse.

Most of us at times get really frustrated with God; sometimes we are deeply upset and confused. Let me share some questions shared with me—some of the things that God has done or not done that really upset people. These were hard to hear. They grabbed my heart.

1.  Why has God not changed the heart of my husband who turned his back on God over 23 years ago?

2.  Why has God allowed our daughter to be the victim of so much evil and tragedy?

3.  God, why won't you heal my son?

4.  How can you leave me to raise four children, alone, while my beloved ex-husband

disgraces us in the streets, not even looking back or thinking of helping in any way?

5.  Why is violent extremism being allowed to run rampant?

6.  Why did our daughter have to be sexually assaulted?

7.  Why did you ignore my prayers to heal my son's addiction and instead, let him die?

8.  God, why did you let my parents get a divorce?

9.  Why did you let Grandpa die?

10. Why were the children in Sandy Hook allowed to die?

11. Why did my sweet, spirited, faithful, obedient, godly mother get cancer twice? Why did she suffer so horribly and die at 69?

I can feel their pain. Maybe you can identify with one or more of these heart cries.

Let's look into God's Word to find help for our burning questions and frustrations.

Habakkuk was so upset that he burst before God in prayer with no typical prelude such as, "Dear Lord," or a confession of sin. He was upset with God. God's answer was so bewildering. It had Habakkuk spinning. What did Habakkuk do with his concerns? He did not go down to his fellow prophets and say, "Hey guys, you are not going to believe what God just told me. How could he do something like this?" He did not run away from God. Habakkuk ran to God.

It's a common mistake to pick up our proverbial toys and walk away. When you are confused or upset, do not stop going to church services, quit reading your Bible or praying. That is a huge mistake. Do not run away from God, but run to God. When you do not understand what God is doing, when life is really confusing, go to God with your questions. That's what Habakkuk did.

## HABAKKUK'S QUESTION

Habakkuk started in a good place, with the character of God. He rehearsed some of what he knew about God.

### God, given who you are

When everything is falling apart and nothing makes sense, you can always fall back on the unchanging character of God. He is steady. In a sea of confusion with waves crashing all around him, Habakkuk clung to the life buoy of God's character. He gave six descriptions of God:

1.  Lord
2.  Active
3.  Eternal
4.  Sovereign
5.  Immortal
6.  Protector

Habakkuk came to God in a personal way. He called him "My sovereign God." He is Habakkuk's God. The image behind "protector" is the Rock. God is our Rock, our refuge, our protection in the storms. We can cling to him. There is no one else like him. God is fundamentally incomparable. So knowing his theology, Habakkuk sprung his big question.

## How could you use the wicked and say nothing?

"God, you are the holy, sovereign God, so how could you empower the Babylonians and use them since they are clearly ruthless, evil people?" Habakkuk presented what he saw as a clear case against God. "Look God, is it not true that you are holy so you cannot condone wrongdoing? True. And you cannot tolerate evil, right? OK, so tell me how in the world you could raise up treacherous people? How could you say nothing while the Babylonians kill, torture and rape innocent people? How does that make any sense? God, you are contradicting yourself."

Habakkuk thought he had God in a logical trap with no apparent way out. If God is moral and powerful, a protector of human life and justice, then how in the world could he use evil people who violently murder and abuse people? Not only was God allowing evil, he was making it happen. It's one thing to punish your people for disobeying, but the injustice of the punishment seemed greater than the disobedience. It's one thing to put your child in timeout; it is another thing all together to smack them in the face. Habakkuk was horrified at the atrocities; at God's indifference, and mostly that God seemed to have caused this to happen.

These people, the Babylonians, were committing what today would be international atrocities for which they would be brought before the International Criminal Court at The Hague to answer for their crimes against humanity. And it got worse: the Babylonians were laughing, enjoying their conquests and taking credit for their success.

They treated people like fish in the sea, animals to be hunted down and captured. Habakkuk's own people were helpless and defenseless like fish on a hook. From historical images, we know the Babylonians sometimes drove a hook through the sensitive lower lips of their captives and strung them like fish in a single file line.[6] They also literally trapped people in nets and held them captive in those nets. Habakkuk was watching a holocaust and God was doing nothing; in fact, God claimed to have sent the Babylonians and was giving them success.

In verse 15, we see that the Babylonians were happy about it. They were gleefully gloating; no remorse, no guilt, and no sorrow for what they had done.

Finally Habakkuk demanded in essence, "How long is this going to go on God? Will the Babylonians just keep on pillaging and raping? Are you going to let them keep on destroying people and killing entire villages? I thought you were the holy, good, powerful God, so why are you doing nothing? How could you possibly have not just allowed, but even enabled, all this evil?! I do not get it."

Habakkuk prepared himself to receive God's answer. He said he would wait like a military guard sitting on a watchtower (2:1, NLT). He prepared himself for God's rebuke and some kind of answer, though I don't think Habakkuk could imagine how God could possibly answer his questions adequately. The contradiction between God's character and what was happening was too obvious and stark. Let's unpack God's answer that begins in 2:2.

## GOD'S ANSWER

God did not rebuke the prophet. He never said that Habakkuk should not have asked those kinds of questions. He was not offended. Rather, he answered with clarity and strength. He gave Habakkuk three practical action steps before giving the heart of his message.

### 1. Write the message: Record it

In those days, serious writing would be recorded on tablets. Recall the Ten Commandments inscribed on tablets of stone. For us today, we have the entire Bible as God's message to us. We should write it on our hearts. Can you imagine copying the entire Bible? It would be one thing to type the entire Bible, another to write it by hand and still another to chisel it onto stone tablets! The application for us is to write God's message into our minds. I encourage you to do that with Habakkuk by reading the entire book several times.

## 2. Witness to the message: Tell it

The message is to be written so that it can be announced. God wants other people to hear it. The message is a witness to what God has decreed. It tells who he is and what will happen. Today, since the coming of Jesus Christ, God calls Christians ambassadors of Jesus' message. We are evangelists, sharing with the world the message of the gospel. We are to tell the message. With whom are you sharing God's wonderful message?

## 3. Wait for the message: It will happen on time

God warns us that the message will not happen as fast as we may want it to happen, but it certainly will come to pass—and it will not arrive late. From our perspective, it often seems that God is taking a long time to act, but from his perspective, the timing is always just right. The Bible says, "The Lord is not slow in keeping his promise, as some understand slowness. Instead he is patient with you, not wanting anyone to perish, but everyone to come to repentance" (2 Peter 3:9, NIV). God is giving people time. I want Jesus to come back, but I want him to wait until some people I love have trusted in him first!

One of the key traits of a mature believer is to live waiting, to live expectantly and patiently for God to fulfill his promises. Jesus says we are to live ready, recognizing that he could come at any time (1 Thessalonians 5:1–8). During difficult days, we need to cultivate the grace of endurance, patiently waiting. Waiting is very hard for me. I hate to wait in a line at the grocery store; it kills me to get in the slow line. Waiting on the phone in voicemail purgatory drives me crazy. I don't like to wait in traffic; I hunt for the faster routes and lanes. Basically, I see waiting as a waste of time, but it is not. God wants us to wait well, trusting his timing in our lives in the little things and also in the much bigger things. God says to "be still and know that I am God" (Psalm 46:10a, NIV).

## KEY TRUTH IN 2:4

We find the key truth of this section in Habakkuk 2:4. Verses 4 and 5 go together by setting up a vivid contrast. The proud, unrighteous people will perish, but the righteous, by faith, will live. Verse 5 amplifies verse 4 by further describing this type of unrighteous person as proud and restless. This person is full of self-confidence, even presumption. Historically, this was the Babylonians and by application, it describes many today who turn away from God in their earthly success. The earth is filled with such people.

Look at the second half of verse 4 because it is one of the most important phrases in the entire Old Testament. Kaiser refers to the Jewish *Talmud* which records this famous remark made by Rabbi Simlai: "Moses gave Israel 613 commandments. David reduced them to eleven [Psalm 15], Micah to 3 [Micah 6:8], Isaiah to 2 [Isaiah 56:1], but Habakkuk to 1 – *'The righteous shall live by his faith* [Hab. 2:4]." Jewish scholars felt these few words summarized God's entire message.[7] Habakkuk 2:4 is quoted three times in the New Testament.

## The righteous will live by faith (fulness)

If you compare a few good English translations, you will see that some say "will live by his **faith**" and others "will live by his **faithfulness**." Why the difference? And what does it matter whether we translate "faith" or "faithfulness"? This is actually a pretty big issue and worth thinking through.

The Hebrew term here is *'emunah.* The standard Hebrew lexicon defines *'emunah* as "firmness, steadfastness, fidelity. 1. lit. *firmness, steadfastness.* 2. *steadfastness.* 3. *faithfulness, trust.*"[8] More than an abstract concept, *'emunah* expresses faith in action.

We have to take into account that Paul quoted Habakkuk 2:4 in Romans and in Galatians to explain that salvation is received by faith as a gift rather than by works of righteousness.

Here is the problem: Is *'emunah* in Habakkuk 2:4 picturing faith in God that makes us righteous or is it picturing faithful living which a righteous person should do to please God? In the immediate context, God was answering Habakkuk's question about the unfair Babylonian invasion that was brutally crushing his people. God's answer was that Habakkuk and his people were to be faithful to him in the face of it, and thus they would live.

However, in biblical theology, the apparent conflict between "by faith" and "by faithfulness" is a false dichotomy. "Faithful living and trust . . . are inextricably bound together."[9] The Hebrew term 'emunah in all its forms and uses encompasses both trust and faithfulness. The conflict between faith and faithfulness is artificial. The Bible does not know of a true faith that is not faithful. And a faithful life comes from trust in our faithful God. "In other words, faith and faithfulness are two sides of the same coin."[10]

I like this illustration by Bruckner in his commentary on Habakkuk: "If I have faith in marriage but am not faithful to my wife, do I keep faith or live by it? Faith is what faith does. . . . Faith as an abstraction or as assent to a principle is not living by faith."[11] We can easily over-emphasize one or the other, either by over-stressing human responsibility to live a faithful life or by focusing on trusting in God to the neglect of faithful obedience to God. In the face of disaster, Habakkuk was not to sink into despair, but to live faithfully to God's

Word trusting in the Lord that what he had promised would certainly happen.

I mentioned that this phrase is quoted three times in the New Testament. We will look at those passages. Paul quoted Habakkuk 2:4 as the theme for his entire amazing book of Romans.

> *For in the gospel the righteousness of God is revealed— a righteousness that is by faith from first to last, just as it is written: "The righteous will live by faith."*
>
> —Romans 1:17, NIV

We are accepted by God through faith in Jesus Christ and then we live by faith. Bruckner explains with this analogy: "Faith flows into faithfulness as naturally as spring water flows into a streambed." There is no conflict between the spring and the stream.[12]

In Galatians, Paul quoted Habakkuk 2:4b to prove that a person is justified before God by faith, not by the Mosaic Law.[13] Paul wrote:

*Clearly no one who relies on
the law is justified before God,
because the righteous will live by
faith.*
                    —Galatians 3:11, NIV

Salvation is only by faith. You cannot work your way into God's graces. You could never do enough good to get into heaven. Rather, salvation is a gift based on what Jesus Christ did on the cross. Your salvation is not free; it is very costly to God. If you have never done so, I urge you to trust in Jesus Christ as your Savior. God will forgive you. He will make you righteous before him by putting Christ's righteousness to your account.

The third and final New Testament quotation of Habakkuk 2:4 comes in the book of Hebrews:

*But my righteous one will live
by faith.*
                    —Hebrews 10:38, NIV

In context, the author is encouraging believers to stay faithful to God through tough trials and difficult experiences. Continue to live by faith, faithfully obeying God's Word.

So what is the point of this text in Habakkuk? In spite of confusing circumstances, live by faith, faithfully following God's Word that will certainly come to pass. God never explained why he was using the Babylonians. I doubt Habakkuk could have understood and neither could we. The point is not to understand everything God does and why, but rather to trust in God and faithfully follow his Word.

Recently I received a prayer letter from my friend Musa Asake, a Christian leader in Nigeria. His situation reminds me of Habakkuk. Musa writes, "The challenge for the church in Nigeria continues to be critical. The Moslem extremist group [Boko Haram] is still busy killing innocent people and burning down places of worship with impunity. We are crying to God on a daily basis, but also bearing in mind that His timing is different from ours and so we will continue to wait on Him; hoping and trusting that this merciless kind of killing will one day stop."

What Musa knows and Habakkuk knew is that God is bigger and greater than we are. His ways are higher, beyond our understanding.

And that's a good thing. We don't worship a
god who fits in our little minds. Practically, God
told Habakkuk to write the message, witness to
the message and wait for the message to be
fulfilled. These instructions apply to us today.
Let's write God's message in our minds and tell
it to others as we wait for Jesus to return.

Habakkuk shows us that we can run to
God with our most difficult questions and
frustrations. In a shaking world, we can rely on
God's unshakeable character. The ultimate
answer to our cry of "Why?" is the everlasting
"Who?" When things are shaking, we trust in
the One who is unshakeable. Read once again
the famous final verses of Habakkuk with
which we close each chapter:

> *When the fig tree does not bud,*
> *and there are no grapes on the vines;*
> *when the olive trees do not produce,*
> *and the fields yield no crops;*
> *when the sheep disappear from the pen,*
> *and there are no cattle in the stalls,*
> *18I will rejoice because of the Lord;*
> *I will be happy because of the God who*
> *delivers me!*
> *19The sovereign Lord is my source of*

*strength.*
*He gives me the agility of a deer;*
*he enables me to negotiate the rugged*
*terrain.*

—Habakkuk 3:17–19

In the next chapter, we will see that God will hold Babylon accountable, as he does all people.

# 3

# GOD, YOU WILL MAKE IT RIGHT!

Sometimes life has a way of shaking our lives; sometimes it shakes our faith. As we learn how to hold on to the unshakeable God when he makes no sense, we're entering into the third section of Habakkuk—the five woes or dooms.

## HABAKKUK

| Chapter 1a | Chapter 1b | Chapter 2 | Chapter 3 |
|---|---|---|---|
| 1:1–11 | 1:12–2:5 | 2:6–20 | 3:1–19 |
| Watch | Wait | Warn | Worship |
| Questions | Faith | Five woes | Praise song |

## HABAKKUK 2:6–20

*"But all these nations will someday taunt him and ridicule him with proverbial sayings:*
*'The one who accumulates what does not belong to him is as good as dead*
*(How long will this go on?)—*
*he who gets rich by extortion!'*
*⁷Your creditors will suddenly attack; those who terrify you will spring into action, and they will rob you.*
*⁸Because you robbed many countries, all who are left among the nations will rob you.*
*You have shed human blood and committed violent acts against lands, cities, and those who live in them.*
*⁹The one who builds his house by unjust gain is as good as dead.*
*He does this so he can build his nest way up high*

and escape the clutches of disaster.
¹⁰Your schemes will bring shame to your
house.
Because you destroyed many nations, you
will self-destruct.
¹¹For the stones in the walls will cry out,
and the wooden rafters will answer back.
¹²The one who builds a city by bloodshed
is as good as dead—
he who starts a town by unjust deeds.
¹³Be sure of this! The Lord who
commands armies has decreed:
The nations' efforts will go up in smoke;
their exhausting work will be for nothing.
¹⁴For recognition of the Lord's sovereign
majesty will fill the earth
just as the waters fill up the sea.

¹⁵"You who force your neighbor to drink
wine are as good as dead—
you who make others intoxicated by
forcing them to drink from the bowl of
your furious anger,
so you can look at their genitals.
¹⁶But you will become drunk with shame,
not majesty.
Now it is your turn to drink and expose

*your uncircumcised foreskin!*
*The cup of wine in the Lord's right hand*
*is coming to you,*
*and disgrace will replace your majestic*
*glory!*
*[17]For you will pay in full for your violent*
*acts against Lebanon;*
*terrifying judgment will come upon you*
*because of the way you destroyed the*
*wild animals living there.*
*You have shed human blood*
*and committed violent acts against*
*lands, cities, and those who live in them.*
*[18]What good is an idol? Why would a*
*craftsman make it?*
*What good is a metal image that gives*
*misleading oracles?*
*Why would its creator place his trust in it*
*and make such mute, worthless things?*
*[19]The one who says to wood, 'Wake up!' is*
*as good as dead—*
*he who says to speechless stone, 'Awake!'*
*Can it give reliable guidance?*
*It is overlaid with gold and silver;*
*it has no life's breath inside it.*
*[20]But the Lord is in his majestic palace.*

*The whole earth is speechless in his presence!"*

Mature faith humbly trusts in the God whom we can never fully understand. In the face of evil and suffering, we trust in the Lord God who will one day fill the earth with his glory.

In the next striking passage, we get a preview of what will happen to those who are unrighteous and proud.

A deep question for the people in Habakkuk's day was how to live faithfully for God while they were being cruelly oppressed by the evil Babylonians. Their cry has been echoed throughout history all the way to today by those who are victims—those oppressed by powerful people who are oftentimes cruel. We think of the Jews in Nazi Germany. We think of slaves in the nineteenth century in America. What about people today who are unjustly mistreated for their faith, their color, their sexuality, their status as felons or for being immigrants? What about people oppressed in North Korea or the Central African Republic or in northern Nigeria? How can we live faithfully while we are suffering?

Our text today gives us insight into how to endure well. It gives victims a voice that transforms them into survivors. It gives hope to the hopeless and peace to those in great pain.

Before we get to the text itself, we need to understand its literary form because this passage is culturally distant from us. I have come to some fresh insights for me that are challenging, partially because they are not familiar.

Let's read the first verse of our passage that previews the rest of the passage. Habakkuk 2:6:

> *But all these nations will*
> *someday taunt him and ridicule*
> *him with proverbial sayings.*

The speaker of these sayings is the nations, those who are being oppressed. They will taunt and ridicule "him." The "him" is the Babylonian tyrant who stands for the nations, which while historical, also represents all proud oppressors. What follows is a taunt song with five stanzas. Each one has the Hebrew word, *Hoy*, which is onomatopoetic. It means woe or doom. It was used during funerals as a wailing lament for the dead. God gave Habakkuk a mock funeral dirge to ridicule the Babylonian oppressors. While it appears that the proud, cruel oppressors were winning the day, the victims sang a song of lament for the soon to be dead. The Babylonians were on the verge of death and didn't know it. The righteous victims by faith would live, but the proud, temporary victors were about to die so they were having a funeral for them in advance.

Babylon looked invincible, as has every great empire in history—but in the end, they all fell.

In a series of five mocking oracles, God gave the victims a powerful voice of hope, justice and victory. Each of the five dooms describes the sin of the ungodly and the corresponding judgment to come. This series of dooms shows that ultimately sin, evil, crime, injustice, oppression and immorality are doomed to destruction. In answer to Habakkuk's questions, God essentially said, "I am on my throne; I do see what's going on and I am going to do something about it in a very serious way." "Vengeance is Mine . . . says the Lord" (Romans 12:19, NKJ).

What's striking to me is that these verses of doom were sung by the victims to their captors. God gives us this strong language as seeds of hope, turning helpless victims into hope-filled survivors. The ungodly proud think they are on top of the mountain, but they will crash while their victims, who seem in bad shape, will actually live forever in God's power. God empowers the victims and gives them a voice.

It seems wrong for us to taunt our enemies or rejoice in their downfall. Where are we ever called to ridicule anyone? It helps to see a parallel passage in Revelation 18 where we see three woes on Babylon who still represents all ungodly, powerful people. In Revelation 18:20, the godly are to rejoice over the fall of Babylon. We learn that it is appropriate to rejoice in justice. In short, it's the plot of many movies—the bad guys lose; the good guys win. And we applaud. Where sin distorts this healthy joy over justice is when it contorts it into revenge and vengeance. We are not to get back at our oppressors or to gloat over their downfall. Rather, we are to rejoice in God's victory over evil. We are to delight in justice being done and all being set right.

By application, we can see three powerful implications of these five dooms: first, they function as a warning to God's people of sins that we must avoid; secondly, they warn the ungodly to repent; and thirdly, they assure us that God will make it all right. We can trust him. We see a correlation to the practical steps from the last section to write the message in our hearts, to witness to the message and to wait for the message.

| GOD'S SECOND ANSWER | THE FIVE DOOMS |
|---|---|
| Write the message | Warn God's people of sins to avoid |
| Witness to the message | Warn the ungodly to repent |
| Wait for the message | Assurance that God will make it all right |

As we walk through the five stanzas, look for ironic lamentation against proud people who think they have built security and are untouchable. Notice how sin will catch up with you. You reap what you sow. Often the punishment will match the sin. The one who builds will be torn down. The one who shames others will be disgraced. Sinners will taste the pain their sin has caused.[14] In Hebrew, this section is filled with many poetic devices that sharpen the point. Even the structure is artistic.

| DOOM 1 | DOOM 2 | **DOOM 3** | DOOM 4 | DOOM 5 |
|--------|--------|------------|--------|--------|
| 2:6–8  | 2:9–11 | 2:12–14    | 2:15–17 | 2:18–20 |
| 2:8    |        | **2:14**   | 2:17   | 2:20   |

The five dooms form two panels of the first and second, and then fourth and fifth, with the third in the middle. The ending lines of the first are repeated as the ending of the fourth, and we find crucial truth at the center in verse 14 and at the end in verse 20. Read Habakkuk 2:6–20 again, listening for God's warnings. In the NET version, the Hebrew, *Hoy*, is translated by "as good as dead."

What's the point of this amazing text? The Lord will judge the ungodly and fill the earth with his glory, so sing truth to warn yourself not to sin, to warn the ungodly of divine doom and to assure yourself that God will make it right. One day, justice will be done. God will vindicate his name and finally set everything right. Let's walk through each doom.

## THE FIRST DOOM
### Greedy people will pay a heavy price
#### VERSES 6—8

Proud people who get rich through legal and illegal means will be attacked by their creditors. Those who have robbed others will be robbed themselves. They exploited others; now they will be exploited. You who have financially victimized others are as good as dead. Your sin has come due. The Bible says, "Do not be deceived: God cannot be mocked. A man reaps what he sows" (Galatians 6:7, NIV).

In our culture of consumerism, materialism and obsession with money and what it can buy, we need to listen to this warning. On the world scene, Americans are correctly viewed as over-consumerists, whether Christians or not.

Notice the one scary word in verse 7, "suddenly." In Hebrew, it means "in the blink of an eye." God is patient a long time and then he is done. Proverbs says, "Whoever remains stiff-necked after many rebukes will suddenly be destroyed—without remedy" (Proverbs 29:1, NIV). We dare not presume on God's patience and mercy. Judgment is coming and when it comes, it will be sudden, even without warning. Do not wait to get your life right with God.

The last line, which will be repeated in verse 17, shows that the Babylonians had violated not only other people, but even the land. They clear-cut forests and wiped out animals. They had not taken care of the world that God gave us. God was not happy. In short, we need to listen to God's warning against our own greed; warn proud people that judgment is coming and be assured that God will make everything right.

## THE SECOND DOOM
Schemers will find shame
VERSES 9—11

The second doom starting in verse 9 highlights those who try to find security in building their empire through their schemes. By their unjust gain described in the first doom, they build their nest way up high, thinking they are creating security and will escape disaster, but they are dead wrong. The whole exercise is one big delusion. Their schemes will not secure their dynasty, but actually will bring shame to their family. Rather than building a secure fortress, they are laying a foundation for their destruction. Wealthy and powerful people try to build legacies of power and influence, often in shady ways.

But God says the very stones in their walls will cry out against them. Their woodwork will answer back against their injustice and proud empire building. With this lament, we warn the ungodly that no matter how wealthy they are, no matter what their retirement investments, they are not secure. With this taunt, we warn ourselves not to be seduced by the temptation to find security in building our nest up high. We must avoid schemes to get rich and find security in this life. Finally we can be assured that God will make all things right. Those proud schemers will find shame. The third doom speaks directly to the empire builders.

## THE THIRD DOOM
*Unjust builders will go up in smoke*
### VERSES 12–13

The Babylonians built their empire on the backs of slaves whom they brutally treated. They thought they had accomplished a great achievement won by their hard work and power, but pride falls hard. God was not impressed. In seeking their own glory, they saw all their efforts go up in smoke. All their human achievements gained by their exhausting work would be for nothing. They built huge temples, fortresses, cities and gardens, wonders of the ancient world. All up in smoke.

Be warned that life is not found in building our little empires. Warn the powerful that all their hard-won achievements will go up in smoke in an instant. God says in verse 13 that we can "be sure of this." The Lord who commands armies has decreed it. It will happen.

Now we come to the first of the two awesome divine truths that give victims supreme confidence. This one comes right at the center of our text. Here's Habakkuk 2:14 in the New International Version: "For the earth will be filled with the knowledge of the glory of the Lord as the waters cover the sea."

## The Lord's supreme majesty will fill the earth
### VERSE 14

The Babylonians and all self-reliant people since them have exchanged the glory of God for their own glory. Rather than living by faith, they are dying by human effort. Pride kills. Faith lives. Be assured, no matter what circumstances look like today, no matter how you are being cruelly oppressed by powerful people, God's glory will fill the earth. The glory of God is his manifest presence, his sovereign majesty. Glory is the outward expression of God's being.

The knowledge of his glory means more than cognitive awareness, it means the personal experience of his supreme majesty. Today, no matter what we are living through, people of faith have the absolute assurance that God's glory will cover the earth and everyone will know his supreme majesty.

The revelation of God's glory on earth is possible because of Jesus Christ who came to show us God's glory. Paul says, "For God, who said, 'Let light shine out of darkness,' made his light shine in our hearts to give us the light of the knowledge of God's glory displayed in the face of Christ" (2 Corinthians 4:6, NIV).

Today we can know some of God's glory through faith in Jesus Christ. Pray that by the Spirit we "may have power, together with all the Lord's holy people, to grasp how wide and long and high and deep is the love of Christ, and to know this love that surpasses knowledge—that you may be filled to the measure of all the fullness of God" (Ephesians 3:18–19, NIV). Then one day, we will see the Lord face to face and personally know his supreme majesty that will fill the earth.

## THE FOURTH DOOM
*Immoral people will be disgraced*
### VERSES 15–17

With graphic language, God mocked the immoral Babylonians. Alcohol and sex have been a bad combination for thousands of years leading to debauchery and shame. Wealthy, powerful people have held drunken parties where people disgraced themselves. As they have treated others, taking advantage of them sexually, so they will pay in full for their acts. Those who have gotten drunk on wine will drink the cup of God's wrath. One possible graphic translation is that they will vomit shame on their glory. Picture that. It's the morning-after ugly toilet experience on a larger scale.

Today in a culture full of addiction and sexual obsession, we need this warning. Sin brings its own terrible reward. Alcohol abuse and immoral sexual activity bring terrible shame and self-destruction. This fourth doom ends by repeating the last line of the first doom in verse 8 as a refrain warning against violence.

## THE FIFTH DOOM
*Idol worshippers will find silent death*
### VERSES 18–19

People who worship idols will discover that they are powerless. Idols cannot speak and they are lifeless—dead. They are futile. Idols are made by human beings and can do nothing.

Today we are quick to worship things other than God. We trust in ourselves, and what we build or buy. In Hebrew, these lines drip with ridicule as the speaker mocks: "Why don't you ask the idol to wake up? It is mute and dead." By great contrast, Yahweh, the true Lord God, speaks, is awake, guides us and gives the breath of life. He is Life and the life-giver.[15] So now we come to the finale, the last powerful line in verse 20: "But the Lord is in his holy temple; let all the earth be silent before him" (Habakkuk 2:20, NIV).

## Be silent before the Lord
### VERSE 20

The Hebrew word for "be silent" is *hāsâh*. It can be translated, "hush," *hāsâh*. Habakkuk calls us to silent reverence, respectful allegiance to the Lord who sits in his majestic palace as the rightful King of the world. When you really open your eyes to see the incomparable God, you are speechless. There are no words to say, but we can fall on our knees in wonder and worship, in trembling trust before the awesome God of all.

In response to Habakkuk's pressing questions, God provides a powerful and surprising response. Our silence before him is not just the silence of reverence, but the recognition that he will judge the ungodly. This silence stands in marked contrast to the frantic business of the ungodly building their empire, disgracing themselves and spending their money on lifeless idols.

God tells us that the righteous will live by faith and faithfulness while the ungodly will reap what they sow. God will make all things right. Until that time, God gives victims the gift of a song that offers warning and hope. It transforms helpless victims into hopeful survivors.

We take these five dooms as a warning to us and to our children against greed, injustice, violence, immorality and trusting in created things. We write them on our hearts. We take these dooms as a warning for the ungodly so we tell them God's message. Be warned: God will bring shame and disgrace on you. You will self-destruct and taste God's wrath.

He will judge the ungodly. The only hope of any human being is to find safety in Jesus Christ our Savior. We have all sinned. We have all pridefully tried to build our own security apart from God. The only hope is faith in the One who came to save us from ourselves, the One who gives life eternally.

While Habakkuk did not get detailed answers as to why God was doing just what he was doing, he learned more about the mysterious ways of God and so have we. We cannot grasp all of God, and that is good. God is God and we are not. He will never fit in our puny little brains.

From this text, we have learned that the Lord will judge the ungodly and fill the earth with his glory so we can sing truth to warn ourselves not to sin, to warn the ungodly of divine doom and to assure ourselves that God will make it right. It is the Lord Almighty, not Babylon, who rules the earth. Even when it looks like the forces of darkness are shutting out all the light, it is merely temporary. God will flood the earth with his brilliant glory.

Habakkuk shows us that we can run to God with our most difficult questions and frustrations. In a shaking world, we can rely on

God's unshakeable character. The ultimate answer to our cry of "Why?" is the everlasting "Who?" When things are shaking, we trust in the One who is unshakeable. Turn to the famous chorus at the end of Habakkuk:

> *When the fig tree does not bud,*
> *and there are no grapes on the vines;*
> *when the olive trees do not produce,*
> *and the fields yield no crops;*
> *when the sheep disappear from the pen,*
> *and there are no cattle in the stalls,*
> *18I will rejoice because of the LORD;*
> *I will be happy because of the God who delivers me!*
> *19The sovereign LORD is my source of strength.*
> *He gives me the agility of a deer;*
> *he enables me to negotiate the rugged terrain.*
> —Habakkuk 3:17–19

In view of chapter 2:20, I think it is only appropriate, before we come to the final chapter of the book, to take a moment to be silent before the Lord.

*Hāsâh.* Silence.

# 4

# GOD, WE WORSHIP YOU!

The big point of Habakkuk comes in the last verse to which we will come as we unpack the final section of the book.

## Habakkuk

| Chapter 1a | Chapter 1b | Chapter 2 | Chapter 3 |
|------------|------------|-----------|-----------|
| 1:1–11 | 1:12–2:5 | 2:6–20 | 3:1–19 |
| Watch | Wait | Warn | Worship |
| Questions | Faith | Five woes | Praise song |

## Habakkuk 3:1—19

*This is a prayer of Habakkuk the prophet:*
*[2]LORD, I have heard the report of what*
*you did;*
*I am awed, LORD, by what you*
*accomplished.*
*In our time repeat those deeds;*
*in our time reveal them again.*
*But when you cause turmoil, remember*
*to show us mercy!*
*[3]God comes from Teman,*
*the sovereign one from Mount Paran.*
*Selah.*
*His splendor covers the skies,*
*his glory fills the earth.*
*[4]He is as bright as lightning;*
*a two-pronged lightning bolt flashes*
*from his hand.*
*This is the outward display of his power.*
*[5]Plague goes before him;*

*pestilence marches right behind him.*
*6He takes his battle position and shakes the earth;*
*with a mere look he frightens the nations.*
*The ancient mountains disintegrate;*
*the primeval hills are flattened.*
*He travels on the ancient roads.*
*7I see the tents of Cushan overwhelmed by trouble;*
*the tent curtains of the land of Midian are shaking.*
*8Is the LORD mad at the rivers?*
*Are you angry with the rivers?*
*Are you enraged at the sea?*
*Is this why you climb into your horse-drawn chariots,*
*your victorious chariots?*
*9Your bow is ready for action;*
*you commission your arrows. Selah.*
*You cause flash floods on the earth's surface.*
*10When the mountains see you, they shake.*
*The torrential downpour sweeps through.*
*The great deep shouts out;*
*it lifts its hands high.*

*¹¹The sun and moon stand still in their courses;*
*the flash of your arrows drives them away,*
*the bright light of your lightning-quick spear.*
*¹²You furiously stomp on the earth,*
*you angrily trample down the nations.*
*¹³You march out to deliver your people,*
*to deliver your special servant.*
*You strike the leader of the wicked nation,*
*laying him open from the lower body to the neck. Selah.*
*¹⁴You pierce the heads of his warriors with a spear.*
*They storm forward to scatter us;*
*they shout with joy as if they were plundering the poor with no opposition.*
*¹⁵But you trample on the sea with your horses,*
*on the surging, raging waters.*

*¹⁶I listened and my stomach churned;*
*the sound made my lips quiver.*
*My frame went limp, as if my bones were decaying,*

*and I shook as I tried to walk.*
*I long for the day of distress*
*to come upon the people who attack us.*
*[17]When the fig tree does not bud,*
*and there are no grapes on the vines;*
*when the olive trees do not produce,*
*and the fields yield no crops;*
*when the sheep disappear from the pen,*
*and there are no cattle in the stalls,*
*[18]I will rejoice because of the LORD;*
*I will be happy because of the God who*
*delivers me!*
*[19]The sovereign LORD is my source of*
*strength.*
*He gives me the agility of a deer;*
*he enables me to negotiate the rugged*
*terrain.*

*(This prayer is for the song leader. It is to*
*be accompanied by stringed*
*instruments.)*

Our encounter with God in Habakkuk melts our confusion into confidence. In the face of suffering, we trust in the Lord who will one day fill the earth with his glory.

In the first two chapters, Habakkuk fix-ated on life's problems; in chapter 3, he focused on the person of God. While the book of Habakkuk began with a question mark, it ends with an exclamation point. The prophet started in frustrated doubt, but he ended in triumphant faith. As we began this book, I invited you to consider the questions you want to ask God. As we conclude, see if you have made progress.

Hebrew scholars consider Habakkuk 3 one of the finest examples of Hebrew poetry. From the first verse, we see the chapter is a prayer. From the last line, we see that it is a song set to music. Most likely it was designed for public worship. In chapter 3, you will see the word *Selah* three times. While we are not sure what it means, it appears to function as a musical notation.

Chapter 3 is a poetic prayer set to music, a hymn declaring that God is coming. This song elaborates the theme of the book in 2:4 that the righteous live by faith and faithfulness. Habakkuk blends historical allusions and natural phenomena to engage our imaginations to see and hear the coming of God as the divine warrior to judge and to deliver. As the divine warrior, he defeats his enemies and shakes the earth. As we enter Habakkuk 3, prepare yourself for elevated poetic language that paints a picture beyond our ability to fully grasp the coming of God.

What's the point of Habakkuk 3? Rejoice in the all-powerful Lord God who will judge the ungodly and deliver his people, and who gives strength today no matter how difficult life becomes. Habakkuk dropped his protest against God. He had progressed beyond his intellectual perplexity to profound worship. Rather than advising God on how to run the universe, he was awed by him. Questions about justice faded before an encounter with God himself. The chapter begins with a request, then describes the coming of God and ends with Habakkuk's response. Let's look at the request. Habakkuk asked God to reveal his power with mercy.

## Request: reveal your power with mercy
### VERSES 1–2

Notice the striking contrast between the first two verses of chapter 1 and the first two verses of chapter 3. Here's the start of chapter 1:

> *The following is the message*
> *which God revealed to Habakkuk*
> *the prophet:*
> *² How long, LORD, must I cry*
> *for help?*
> *But you do not listen!*
> *I call out to you, "Violence!"*
> *But you do not intervene!*
> —Habakkuk 1:1–2

Contrast that with where he is now in chapter 3:

> *This is a prayer of Habakkuk the*
> *prophet:*
> *²LORD, I have heard the report of*
> *what you did;*
> *I am awed, LORD, by what you*
> *accomplished.*
> *In our time repeat those deeds;*

*in our time reveal them again.*
*But when you cause turmoil,*
*remember to show us mercy!*
—Habakkuk 3:1–2

Gone was the need to figure it all out; gone was his concern with his own immediate problems. He recognized that God is God and he was not. God can do whatever he wants and what he does is ultimately best in the big picture and in the long run. Habakkuk simply prayed for God to reveal his power, his great deeds, and to do so with mercy. This is similar to praying, "Your kingdom come; your will be done" (Matthew 6:10a, NIV). His concern had shifted from himself and his issues to God and his will.

Habakkuk was awed by what he had heard about who God is and what he had done and will do. The Hebrew word for "awe" includes the aspect of healthy fear in the sense of the fear of the Lord. In the midst of turmoil, Habakkuk asked God to remember to show mercy to his people, which of course God always does, as he promises. In verse 3, Habakkuk poetically depicted the coming of God.

## God comes to earth
VERSES 3—15

Verse 3 opens with the line, "God comes from Teman." He is on the earth. Just hold for a minute on the first two words: "God comes." Consider who God is. The Almighty, glorious, incomparable God, the I AM. There is no one like him. There is only one God. He is the sovereign One. Follow as we move through verses 3–15 experiencing God coming.

In a collage of images, Habakkuk opens our eyes and ears to experience God coming by blending historical allusions to his previous mighty acts with natural phenomenon, such as lightening, plagues and earthquakes. His coming is awesome, frightening and over-whelming as well as a cause for rejoicing. This is a theophany, a physical manifestation of God's presence on earth.

God's splendor covers the skies and his glory fills the earth. Skies and earth together symbolize everything. He fills the universe with his presence. He is as bright as lightening or a brilliant sunrise.

I can remember an early morning down at Port Aransas on the Texas coast when my wife, Tamara, and I got up to see the sunrise. We sat on the beach in the dark watching as the light pushed back the darkness, the first rays appeared and then a ball of fire crept over the horizon. Soon we were shielding our eyes and finally we could no longer look at the sun in all its brilliance. So it is with God.

As a mighty warrior, he holds lightning bolts in his hands, displaying his great power to crush his enemies. As he takes his battle position, he shakes the earth itself and a mere look terrifies the nations. How would you like to face almighty God on the other side of a battlefield? Ancient mountains disintegrate and primeval hills are flattened. Mountains symbolize stability and permanence.

When I am in the Rocky Mountains, I am aware of how small I am, awestruck by the massiveness of the mountains. But they grovel before the coming of God who made them all.

In verse 8, Habakkuk moved to personal address. With historical allusions to the Exodus, Mount Sinai and the conquest of Canaan, Habakkuk depicts God the warrior in his victorious chariots with his bow ready for action. Floods covered the earth, mountains shook and storms rained down as the great deep itself shouted out. Earth, water and sky cried out and served God as weapons in his hands since he is the Creator-Warrior. The sun and the moon stood still as the flash of God's arrows outshone them both, as the bright light of his lightning-quick spear flashed. He furiously stomped the earth and trampled down the nations.

In verse 13, we see that his judgment accomplishes our deliverance. God marched out to deliver his people, his special servants. He struck the leader of the wicked nation who represents all evil tyrants, including ultimately the Antichrist and the Devil. Our divine warrior, almighty God, is the victor as he pierced the heads of the enemy warriors and trampled the sea with his horses on the surging, raging waters. As God has fought for his people before, so he will again once and for all.

This prayer-song remembers what God has done and anticipates what he will do. God's dramatic coming removes the dangerous illusion that he is disengaged or does not care. We dare not assume that God is not aware of what is happening in our lives and in our world. We must live ready for his return at any time. As God delivered his people from Pharaoh and the Egyptians, and later the Assyrians and also the Babylonians, so he will deliver us from Satan and from death itself. Remembering what God has done in the past anchors us in the present as we faithfully wait for his coming in the future. How did Habakkuk respond to this overwhelming vision of God's coming?

## HABAKKUK'S RESPONSE

We see Habakkuk's report of his response.

> *I listened and my stomach*
> *churned;*
> *the sound made my lips quiver.*
> *My frame went limp, as if my*
> *bones were decaying,*
> *and I shook as I tried to walk.*
> *I long for the day of distress*
> *to come upon the people who*
> *attack us.*
> —Habakkuk 3:16

We cannot encounter the living God mildly. Habakkuk was shaken and so would we be. God's coming is at once terrifying and overwhelming and reassuring as he judges and delivers. Habakkuk longed for the Lord to come; for final justice; for God's victory over his enemies.

For Babylon, it came quickly. Their empire was short-lived, only 87 years. In 559 BC, the Medes and the Persians took over Babylon under King Belshazzar (referenced in Daniel 5) with the writing on the wall. The Babylonians were done.

All human empires will be short-lived. Evil is running wild now, but one day it will be done. We can live today by faith knowing what tomorrow is bringing. God is coming.

In 3:17, Habakkuk honestly faced very difficult circumstances. Judah's main economy was agrarian. Therefore, in mentioning fig trees, grapes, olive trees, fields, sheep and cattle, he describes their food source and their economy. These include necessities such as milk and meat. Habakkuk accepted scarcity as a consequence of sin, his nation's and other's. God warned this would happen if they turned away from him. Scarcity and suffering show us our need for God. Our inner joy does not depend on outward prosperity. God's blessing is not measured by material wealth (Ephesians 1:2–4; Philippians 4:11–13).

As we wait in faithful expectation during difficult circumstances, we can rejoice because of the Lord. Read these wonderful verses:

> *I will rejoice because of the LORD;*
> *I will be happy because of the God*
> *who delivers me!*
> *The sovereign LORD is my source*
> *of strength.*
> *He gives me the agility of a deer;*
> *he enables me to negotiate the*
> *rugged terrain.*
> —Habakkuk 3:18–19

The complaining prophet was transformed into the rejoicing prophet. Even in the most horrifying circumstances, Habakkuk said, "I will rejoice because of the Lord."

## Rejoice because of the Lord

Habakkuk did not minimize the difficulties or the pain as if this was just spilled milk. He did not close his eyes and just grit it out or merely try to look on the bright side. This was not mere resignation to fate, nor was Habakkuk trying to grin and bear it. Out of his unconditional trust in God, he rejoiced in the Lord. He knew that God is the Lord. He is on his throne. He cares. He will keep his Word.

One day evil will finally be dealt with; all will be set right. God will deliver his people. This joy is not superficial happiness or a cheerful personality—just put on a happy face. This is the deep well of joy that comes from a heart centered on God himself. It is supernatural. It is grounded and springs from a personal relationship with the living God that can never be stripped away from us.

The New Testament says we can consider it pure joy when we encounter trials (James 1). In spite of great difficulties, we can greatly rejoice because of the praise, glory and honor to come when Jesus returns (1 Peter 1). Habakkuk mentioned three powerful truths about the Lord. First, we can rejoice in the Lord who delivers us.

## Who delivers us

God's coming is described as shaking the earth.
God came to earth in the incarnation when
Jesus became a human being. In the cross, we
see judgment and salvation unite in one act,
and through Jesus' death, death died. Great
suffering brought great deliverance.

In the end of history, Jesus Christ will
return as the King of Kings with a sword and he
will trample the nations in his righteous wrath
(Revelation 19). His judgment will bring salvation to his people, delivering us once and for all
from the Devil and evil. Death will be no more.
God judges for the sake of his people and for
his name. When Jesus died on the cross, the
earth shook and darkness covered the sky. God
delivers us through the sacrifice of his Son. So
today, we can find joy by trusting in Jesus
Christ.

God promises to deliver us when we trust
in Jesus Christ as Savior. Then you are saved.
Then you can know deep joy in the midst of
great tragedy and you can anticipate ultimate
joy ahead for you. If you have never done so, I
urge you to trust in Jesus Christ. Let someone
else know of your decision. Not only is the Lord

the One who delivers us, but he is also the One who is our strength.

## Who is our strength

This line at the beginning of 3:19 is the centerpiece of Habakkuk's declaration: "The sovereign LORD; is my source of strength." This affirmation stands in great contrast to 1:11 where we read that for the Babylonians, their own strength was their god. In a few short years, they were destroyed by the Persians.

In time, we will reign forever with the all-powerful God who is our strength.

We dare not look to ourselves for strength, especially in the really hard times when there are no grapes on the vines and the fields yield no crops. Habakkuk had every reason not to rejoice, but he knew that no matter how bad life got, God is our source of joy and strength. Nehemiah said, "The joy of the LORD is your strength" (Nehemiah 8:10, NIV). The apostle Paul declared that no matter what the circumstances, whether in need or with plenty, whether well fed or hungry, he was content because he could do all things through him who gives him strength, the Lord God (Philippians 4:11–13). Not only does the Lord deliver us and he is our strength, but he is the One who enables us to negotiate the rugged terrain.

## Negotiate the rugged terrain

The poetic imagery of a deer pictures strength, surefootedness, beauty and speed, bounding over rugged terrain with joy. The Lord gives us strength to bound over rugged terrain like a deer. The person of faith in God's strength can rejoice in the Lord who delivers us and enables us to negotiate the rugged terrain of life. The apostle Paul and his co-worker, Silas, sitting in a dark, stinking, nasty Roman prison cell, sang joyful praises to God (Acts 16:25).

This is a supernatural reality available to God's children by the power of his Spirit. Remember your questions and frustrations, your issues with God. Even though your circumstances do not change, when the Almighty, warrior-Savior God is your strength, you can joyfully handle life's worst trials and tragedies. Habakkuk started in the pits but he ended on the mountaintops, even though his circumstances had not changed at all.

While God does not usually answer our questions because we would not understand the answers, he does satisfy our souls. He is with us and gives us all we need for today while assuring us that he is coming to judge the world and rescue his people. While our circumstances often do not change, chapter 3 teaches us that we can rejoice in the All-Powerful Lord God who will judge the ungodly and deliver his people, and who gives strength today no matter how difficult life becomes.

A book beginning with complaint and distress ends in joy. Habakkuk laid down his own preferences and perspectives for God himself. The anxious prophet became the adoring prophet. Habakkuk turned from grumbling to glorifying. He stopped moaning over his problems and began singing God's praise. His confusion melted into confidence. How has God changed you in the course of studying Habakkuk?

In this confusing time between the resurrection and the return, where evil still runs rampant and terrible suffering happens, we rejoice in the Lord who delivers us, who is our strength and enables us to negotiate the rugged terrain.  God tells us that the righteous will live by faith and faithfulness while the ungodly will reap what they sow. God will make all things right.

Until that time, we faithfully wait for the Lord to come. We rejoice in the Lord. It is the Lord Almighty, not Babylon, who rules the earth. God will flood the earth with his brilliant glory. God is not primarily committed to our prosperity on this earth. He is interested in our faithfulness to him.

Habakkuk shows us that we can run to God with our most difficult questions. In a shaking world, we can rely on God's unshake-able character. The ultimate answer to our cry of "Why?" is the everlasting "Who?" When our lives are shaking like a leaf in the storm, we trust in the One who is unshakeable. Read again the famous end of Habakkuk with which we close each chapter:

> When the fig tree does not bud,
> and there are no grapes on the vines;
> when the olive trees do not produce,
> and the fields yield no crops;
> when the sheep disappear from the pen,

*and there are no cattle in the stalls,*
*18I will rejoice because of the LORD;*
*I will be happy because of the God who*
*delivers me!*
*19The sovereign LORD is my source of*
*strength.*
*He gives me the agility of a deer;*
*he enables me to negotiate the rugged*
*terrain.*

—Habakkuk 3:17–19

# STUDY GUIDE

# WHY, GOD?!

## HABAKKUK 1:1—11

 **Pray**

Prepare your heart and mind before engaging God's Word. Take a moment to pray about questions in your life and issues arising from the Scripture you are studying.

# W Work the issue: *What's really at stake?*

The biblical author is usually addressing a question, issue or problem. At any given moment in our lives, we are facing difficulties, asking questions and trying to make decisions. Your study will be more transforming if you take time to consider what is at stake in the passage and what is currently at stake in your life to which the passage may speak.

Quickly scan the passage considering what underlying issues may be present. Reflecting on what the author might be addressing in his time, what about you today? What questions does this text raise in your own mind? What do you wonder about?

Most of us have cried out to God for help. We've been frustrated that God does not seem to hear our prayers or intervene in a situation where we certainly think we would intervene if we were God. What questions would you like to ask God similar to Habakkuk's? How has God frustrated you by what he has or has not done?

What's at stake? What is the central issue or issues being addressed? What is the biggest issue for yourself?

▬▬▬▬▬▬▬▬▬▬▬▬▬▬▬▬▬

WRITE DOWN THE MAIN ISSUE(S).

## I Investigate Scripture: *What does God say?*

Read the passage slowly underlining what seems important to you. You will benefit from reading it several times. Mark key words. Notice who is speaking in each section. I encourage you to engage God in his Word. A good way to do that is to compare several English translations of the Bible.

For our study of Habakkuk, we are going to work mainly from the NET version, the New

English Translation because I think it does a good job translating this book and exposes you to an excellent translation you might not have used. You can access it for free along with all its extensive notes on Bible.org, one of the best Bible study websites on the Internet.

To easily compare various English translations, I recommend YouVersion as a good Bible reading app. In your study of Habakkuk, it will help you to compare the New International Version (NIV), English Standard Version (ESV), Holman Christian Standard Bible (HCSB) and New Living Translation (NLT) especially for a line or verse that is hard to understand.

Notice that the first four verses of the book are Habakkuk's pointed questions. Then without introduction, in verse 5 God begins to give his shocking answer. This section ends with a stinger in the last phrase.

The following is the message which God revealed to Habakkuk the prophet:

## HABAKKUK 1:1—11

*The following is the message which God revealed to*

*Habakkuk the prophet:*

*² How long, Lord, must I cry for help?*
*But you do not listen!*
*I call out to you, "Violence!"*
*But you do not intervene!*
*³ Why do you force me to witness*
*injustice?*
*Why do you put up with wrongdoing?*
*Destruction and violence confront me;*
*conflict is present and one must endure*
*strife.*
*⁴ For this reason the law lacks power,*
*and justice is never carried out.*
*Indeed, the wicked intimidate the*
*innocent.*
*For this reason justice is perverted.*

*⁵ "Look at the nations and pay attention!*
*You will be shocked and amazed!*
*For I will do something in your lifetime*
*that you will not believe even though you*
*are forewarned.*
*⁶ Look, I am about to empower the*
*Babylonians,*
*that ruthless and greedy nation.*
*They sweep across the surface of the*

earth,
seizing dwelling places that do not
belong to them.
⁷ They are frightening and terrifying;
they decide for themselves what is right.
⁸ Their horses are faster than leopards
and more alert than wolves in the desert.
Their horses gallop,
their horses come a great distance;
like a vulture they swoop down quickly to
devour their prey.
⁹ All of them intend to do violence;
every face is determined.
They take prisoners as easily as one
scoops up sand.
¹⁰ They mock kings
and laugh at rulers.
They laugh at every fortified city;
they build siege ramps and capture them.
¹¹ They sweep by like the wind and pass
on.
But the one who considers himself a god
will be held guilty."

- What questions did Habakkuk pose to God?

- What upset Habakkuk?

- How did Habakkuk analyze the problem?

- How did God introduce his answer in verse 4? Rewrite his introduction in your own words.

- What was God's answer to Habakkuk?

- Summarize how God described the Babylonians in verses 6–11.

- What did God imply in the final line of verse 11?

## S Seek counsel: *What do wise people say?*

Read chapter 1 or watch a video presentation of this chapter.  Access the QR (Quick Response) code that can be read by many smart devices using a scanning app. It allows you to immediately watch the  video. If you do not have a QR code reader, you can access the same material at https://vimeo/99049565.  To the extent you have time and ability, read the relevant section from one of the recommended studies. Also check out the resources available on Bible.org.

## D Develop your response: *What do I think*?

- What is the main point of the passage? Take some time to think through and write down a one-sentence statement of the main point.

- From this biblical text, how is God answering your questions in the "Work the issue" section?

- What do you believe the Spirit of God is impressing on you to do in response to this passage? This could be a change in your thoughts about God, an attitude to transform or an action to take.

## ◉ Openly discuss: *What do we think?*

When you meet with your friend or group, walk through the following questions together but do not be limited by them. Prayerfully allow the Spirit of God to guide your conversation as you seek God together in his Word.

1. Have you ever heard of Habakkuk? Read this book? No matter what they might be, what were your early thoughts about this book before starting our study?

2. Has there been a time in your life when God seemed silent—when he was apparently not answering your prayers? How did (or do) you feel toward God in that situation? Can you relate to Habakkuk?

3. In your own words, how would you express Habakkuk's questions and accusations to God in verses 1–4? What upset him?

4. What hard questions would you like to ask God? What has God done, or not done, that upsets you?

5. What was God's answer to Habakkuk (see verses 6–11)?

6. In the last line of verse 11, what did God say to the Babylonians? How is guilt a universal human problem?

7. Going beyond Habakkuk 1, how does God deal with the problem of human guilt?

Read together the wonderful affirmation in the last three verses of the book: Habakkuk 3:17–19.

# M Move to action: *What will I do?*

In reflecting on your study of Habakkuk 1:1–11, how will you move to action? God calls us not just to know his Word, but also to obey it, to be transformed by it through his Spirit. How do you believe God wants to change you through this text? Write down what you will do differently. This could be a transformation in your mind, in your heart, in your actions or in a relationship with another person.

# HOW COULD YOU, GOD?

## HABAKKUK 1:12–2:5

 **Pray**

 **Work the issue:** *What's really at stake?*

This step is often overlooked, but your study will be more transforming if you take time to consider what is at stake in the passage and what is currently at stake in your life to which the passage may speak.

Quickly scan the passage considering what underlying issues may be present. What deeper questions are at play? Related to what the author might be addressing in his day, what about you in your context? What questions does this text raise in your own mind? What do you wonder about?

Most of us have felt frustrated by God's apparent answer to our prayers. Things sometimes seem worse. How has God frustrated you by what he has or has not done in response to your requests? Habakkuk did not understand how what God was doing fit with what he understood God's character to be. It did not make sense to him. How has God not made sense to you?

What did God say, and what did God not explain to Habakkuk that can help us? God responded to Habakkuk in what is perhaps the most famous verse in the entire book, Habakkuk 2:4, quoted three times in the New Testament.

What's at stake? What is the central issue or issues being addressed? What is the biggest issue for yourself?

WRITE DOWN THE MAIN ISSUE(S).

---

## I Investigate Scripture: *What does God say?*

Read the passage slowly, underlining what seems important to you. Mark key words. Notice who is speaking in each section and who is being addressed. Mark each of Habakkuk's questions. Note each description of God.

### HABAKKUK 1:12—2:5

*Lord, you have been active from ancient times;*

*my sovereign God, you are immortal.*
*Lord, you have made them your*
*instrument of judgment.*
*Protector, you have appointed them as*
*your instrument of punishment.*
*¹³You are too just to tolerate evil;*
*you are unable to condone wrongdoing.*
*So why do you put up with such*
*treacherous people?*
*Why do you say nothing when the wicked*
*devour those more righteous than they*
*are?*
*¹⁴You made people like fish in the sea,*
*like animals in the sea that have no ruler.*
*¹⁵The Babylonian tyrant pulls them all up*
*with a fishhook;*
*he hauls them in with his throw net.*
*When he catches them in his dragnet,*
*he is very happy.*
*¹⁶Because of his success he offers*
*sacrifices to his throw net*
*and burns incense to his dragnet;*
*for because of them he has plenty of food,*
*and more than enough to eat.*
*¹⁷Will he then continue to fill and empty*
*his throw net?*

*Will he always destroy nations and spare
none?
2 I will stand at my watch post;
I will remain stationed on the city wall.
I will keep watching, so I can see what he
says to me
and can know how I should answer
when he counters my argument.*

*²The Lord responded:
"Write down this message! Record it
legibly on tablets,
so the one who announces it may read it
easily.
³For the message is a witness to what is
decreed;
it gives reliable testimony about how
matters will turn out.
Even if the message is not fulfilled right
away, wait patiently;
for it will certainly come to pass—it will
not arrive late.
⁴Look, the one whose desires are not
upright will faint from exhaustion,
but the person of integrity will live
because of his faithfulness.*

*5Indeed, wine will betray the proud,*
*restless man!*
*His appetite is as big as Sheol's;*
*like death, he is never satisfied.*
*He gathers all the nations;*
*he seizes all peoples.*

- What did Habakkuk affirm about God's character?

- What questions did Habakkuk have for God?

- How did Habakkuk describe the Babylonians?

- In short, what seems to be Habakkuk's frustration with God? In other words, what did not make sense to him?

- How did Habakkuk prepare for God's answer in 2:1?

- What several things did God tell Habakkuk to do (2:2–3)?

- Why was Habakkuk to write down the message?

- What contrast do you see in verse 4? How does verse 5 amplify the first half of verse 4?

- Look up and read the three places in the New Testament that quote Habakkuk 2:4—Romans 1:17; Galatians 3:11; Hebrews 10:38. How do these authors each use the quotation from Habakkuk? (Note: Their uses are not the same.)

## S Seek counsel: *What do wise people say?*

Read chapter 2 or watch a video presentation
of this chapter. Access the QR
(Quick Response) code that
can be read by many smart
devices using a scanning app. It
allows you to immediately
watch the video. If you do not have a QR code
reader, you can access the same material at
https://vimeo/99050321. To the extent you
have time and ability, read the relevant section
from one of the recommended studies. Also
check out the resources available on Bible.org.

## D Develop your response: *What do I think?*

- In essence, what is God telling us in this
  text? What is the main point of the passage?
  Take some time to think through and write
  down a one-sentence statement of the main
  point.

- How did God answer and not answer Habakkuk's questions? Then put Habakkuk 2:4 in your own words. What is God saying to us in that verse?

- Initially what do you believe the Spirit of God is impressing you to do in response to this passage? This could be a change in your thoughts about God, an attitude to transform, or an action to take. You will refine your response when you get to the "Move to action" section.

## [O] **Openly discuss:** *What do we think?*

1. When have you had your faith in God shaken? What happened? What are some of your most difficult questions you want to ask God about what he does or does not do?

2. What does Habakkuk say about God's character in 1:12–13? Which of these traits of God are most important to you right now?

3. What was Habakkuk's complaint to God? How do we ask similar questions today? How does God at times not make sense to you?

4. God gave Habakkuk three practical action steps (in the NET version each step starts with "W"). What are they? What could it look like today to do each of these?

5. What are connections between "faith" and "faithfulness"? What does it mean to "live by faith(fulness)"?

6. How do the New Testament writers each use Habakkuk 2:4 in the following verses?

   Romans 1:17
   Galatians 3:11
   Hebrews 10:38

7. Read aloud the final affirmation in Habakkuk 3:17–19. You might want to read it in several translations.

# M Move to action: *What will I do*?

In reflecting on your study of Habakkuk 1:12–2:4, how will you move to action? God calls us not just to know his Word, but also to obey it, to be transformed by it through his Spirit. How do you need to live by faith/faithfulness? Write down what you will do in response to the Word of God. What is the Spirit of God impressing on you?

# GOD, YOU WILL MAKE IT RIGHT!

## HABAKKUK 2:6–20

 **Pray**

# W Work the issue: *What's really at stake?*

As we look at our own society and the state of the world, we see major problems. I wonder what God sees. God told Habakkuk what he saw and what he would do with Babylon. Are there similarities to our problems today?

Verses 2:14 and 2:20 rise up like mountains of divine truth regarding who God is and what he will do one day. How do you view the future?

What's at stake? What is the central issue or issues being addressed? What is the biggest issue for yourself?

WRITE DOWN THE MAIN ISSUE(S).

## I  Investigate Scripture: *What does God say?*

Read the passage slowly, marking what seems important to you. Mark repeated words or phrases. Use brackets or another device to indicate the five stanzas in this passage. Because this passage is full of poetic language, as you compare translations, you will find that they tend to differ here more than in other sections in Habakkuk.

### HABAKKUK 2:6–20

*"But all these nations will someday taunt him*
*and ridicule him with proverbial sayings:*
*'The one who accumulates what does not*
*belong to him is as good as dead*
*(How long will this go on?)—*
*he who gets rich by extortion!'*
*⁷Your creditors will suddenly attack;*
*those who terrify you will spring into*
*action, and they will rob you.*
*⁸Because you robbed many countries,*
*all who are left among the nations will*
*rob you.*

*You have shed human blood*
*and committed violent acts against*
*lands, cities, and those who live in them.*
*⁹The one who builds his house by unjust*
*gain is as good as dead.*
*He does this so he can build his nest way*
*up high*
*and escape the clutches of disaster.*
*¹⁰Your schemes will bring shame to your*
*house.*
*Because you destroyed many nations, you*
*will self-destruct.*
*¹¹For the stones in the walls will cry out,*
*and the wooden rafters will answer back.*
*¹²The one who builds a city by bloodshed*
*is as good as dead—*
*he who starts a town by unjust deeds.*
*¹³Be sure of this! The Lord who*
*commands armies has decreed:*
*The nations' efforts will go up in smoke;*
*their exhausting work will be for nothing.*
*¹⁴For recognition of the Lord's sovereign*
*majesty will fill the earth*
*just as the waters fill up the sea.*

*¹⁵"You who force your neighbor to drink*
*wine are as good as dead—*

*you who make others intoxicated by*
*forcing them to drink from the bowl of*
*your furious anger,*
*so you can look at their genitals.*
*¹⁶But you will become drunk with shame,*
*not majesty.*
*Now it is your turn to drink and expose*
*your uncircumcised foreskin!*
*The cup of wine in the Lord's right hand*
*is coming to you,*
*and disgrace will replace your majestic*
*glory!*
*¹⁷For you will pay in full for your violent*
*acts against Lebanon;*
*terrifying judgment will come upon you*
*because of the way you destroyed the*
*wild animals living there.*
*You have shed human blood*
*and committed violent acts against*
*lands, cities, and those who live in them.*
*¹⁸What good is an idol? Why would a*
*craftsman make it?*
*What good is a metal image that gives*
*misleading oracles?*
*Why would its creator place his trust in it*
*and make such mute, worthless things?*
*¹⁹The one who says to wood, 'Wake up!' is*

*as good as dead—*
*he who says to speechless stone, 'Awake!'*
*Can it give reliable guidance?*
*It is overlaid with gold and silver;*
*it has no life's breath inside it.*
*[20]But the Lord is in his majestic palace.*
*The whole earth is speechless in his*
*presence!"*

- In looking at the introduction to this section in verse 6, who will speak these words? When? To whom?

- What short phrase do you see repeated five times? Check out a few other translations. How do they translate this same line?

- How are some of the judgments in each of the five "dooms" similar to the sins of the one being judged?

- Give a brief heading to each of the five dooms summarizing each one in a short phrase.

- How do 2:14 and 2:20 stand out as unique in this passage?

- What will happen to those getting drunk and being sexually immoral?

- Paraphrase Habakkuk's critique of idols.

- How does the earth respond to God in 2:20? When will that happen? How should we respond to God today?

## S Seek counsel: *What do wise people say?*

Read chapter 3 or watch a video presentation
of this chapter. Access the QR
(Quick Response) code that can
be read by many smart devices
using a scanning app. It allows
you to immediately watch the
video. If you do not have a QR code reader, you
can access the same material at
https://vimeo.com/99050886. To the extent
you have time and ability, read the relevant
section from one of the recommended studies.
Also check out the resources available on
Bible.org.

## D Develop your response: *What do I think?*

- In essence, what is God telling us in this
  text? What is the main point of the passage?
  Write down a one-sentence statement of
  the main point.

- Why is God going to judge Babylon and how will he do it?




- Initially how do you believe the Spirit of God is moving you to respond to this passage? How are you guilty of some of the same types of things that Babylon did? Of what could you repent? How do God's promises in 2:14 and 2:20 impact you? You will refine your response when you get to the "Move to action" section.

## ◉ Openly discuss: *What do we think?*

1.  When in your life have you felt shaken by the storms of life? What is shaking you now?

3.  How does verse 6 characterize this passage? Who is speaking to whom? What kind of literature is this?

3.  Habakkuk gives us five stanzas each with a "doom" or "woe" for the Babylonians. Who could the Babylonians represent today? From each doom, we can hear a warning for us to avoid sin; a warning for the ungodly that sin will be judged and an assurance that God will make things right. Identify the kinds of sins being pointed out, and the punishment coming. Then consider what warning we need to take for ourselves in regard to each doom.

    a. First Doom (verses 6b–8)

    b. Second Doom (verses 9–11)

   c. Third Doom (verses 12–14)

   d. Fourth Doom (verses 15–17)

   e. Fifth Doom (verses 18–20)

4. What assurance can we see in the center of our passage (verse 14)? How does this truth give you confidence today?

5. What is the ultimate response in the last verse (20)? How can we respond that way today?

6. How has God answered Habakkuk? And how can we apply his answer to ourselves today?

7. Read Habakkuk 3:17–19 (NET) aloud.

## M Move to action: *What will I do?*

In reflecting on your study of Habakkuk 2:5–20, how will you move to action? How do you believe God wants to transform you through this text? Write down what you will do differently. This could be a transformation in your mind, in your heart, in your actions or in a relationship with another person. Refine your answer to question 3 in "Develop your response."

# GOD, WE WORSHIP YOU!

## HABAKKUK 3:1–19

 **Pray**

## W Work the issue: *What's really at stake*?

Sometimes we wonder what it might be like for God to appear on earth. This text opens our eyes to see the coming of God. Habakkuk was overwhelmed. I wonder how we would respond.

What kinds of prayers do you pray? This third chapter of Habakkuk is a prayer unlike any most of us have prayed. It ends with the famous declaration that competes with 2:4 as the most memorable part of Habakkuk.

What issues does the final declaration address? What questions does it answer?

What's at stake? What is the central issue or issues being addressed? What is the biggest issue for yourself?

WRITE DOWN THE MAIN ISSUE(S).

# ▋ **Investigate Scripture:** *What does God say?*

Read the passage slowly, underlining what
seems important to you. Notice the structure
from the introductory line, to the prayer
proper and to Habakkuk's response in his final
declaration. Mark the different sections. Note
that *Selah* is most likely a musical notation.

## HABAKKUK 3:1—19

---

*This is a prayer of Habakkuk the prophet:*
*²LORD, I have heard the report of what*
*you did;*
*I am awed, LORD, by what you*
*accomplished.*
*In our time repeat those deeds;*
*in our time reveal them again.*
*But when you cause turmoil, remember*
*to show us mercy!*
*³God comes from Teman,*
*the sovereign one from Mount Paran.*
*Selah.*
*His splendor covers the skies,*
*his glory fills the earth.*
*⁴He is as bright as lightning;*
*a two-pronged lightning bolt flashes*

*from his hand.*
*This is the outward display of his power.*
*⁵Plague goes before him;*
*pestilence marches right behind him.*
*⁶He takes his battle position and shakes*
*the earth;*
*with a mere look he frightens the nations.*
*The ancient mountains disintegrate;*
*the primeval hills are flattened.*
*He travels on the ancient roads.*
*⁷I see the tents of Cushan overwhelmed*
*by trouble;*
*the tent curtains of the land of Midian*
*are shaking.*
*⁸Is the Lᴏʀᴅ mad at the rivers?*
*Are you angry with the rivers?*
*Are you enraged at the sea?*
*Is this why you climb into your horse-*
*drawn chariots,*
*your victorious chariots?*
*⁹Your bow is ready for action;*
*you commission your arrows. Selah.*
*You cause flash floods on the earth's*
*surface.*
*¹⁰When the mountains see you, they*
*shake.*
*The torrential downpour sweeps*

*through.*
*The great deep shouts out;*
*it lifts its hands high.*
*[11] The sun and moon stand still in their*
*courses;*
*the flash of your arrows drives them*
*away,*
*the bright light of your lightning-quick*
*spear.*
*[12] You furiously stomp on the earth,*
*you angrily trample down the nations.*
*[13] You march out to deliver your people,*
*to deliver your special servant.*
*You strike the leader of the wicked*
*nation,*
*laying him open from the lower body to*
*the neck. Selah.*
*[14] You pierce the heads of his warriors*
*with a spear.*
*They storm forward to scatter us;*
*they shout with joy as if they were*
*plundering the poor with no opposition.*
*[15] But you trample on the sea with your*
*horses,*
*on the surging, raging waters.*

*16I listened and my stomach churned;*
*the sound made my lips quiver.*
*My frame went limp, as if my bones were*
*decaying,*
*and I shook as I tried to walk.*
*I long for the day of distress*
*to come upon the people who attack us.*
*17When the fig tree does not bud,*
*and there are no grapes on the vines;*
*when the olive trees do not produce,*
*and the fields yield no crops;*
*when the sheep disappear from the pen,*
*and there are no cattle in the stalls,*
*18I will rejoice because of the LORD;*
*I will be happy because of the God who*
*delivers me!*
*19The sovereign LORD is my source of*
*strength.*
*He gives me the agility of a deer;*
*he enables me to negotiate the rugged*
*terrain.*

*(This prayer is for the song leader. It is to*
*be accompanied by stringed*
*instruments.)*

- From the first and last verses, what do we know about the kind of literature this passage is?

- How did Habakkuk initially respond to God and what did he ask of God in 3:2?

- Notice the opening of verse 3, "God comes." How did Habakkuk poetically depict the coming of God in the following verses (3–15)?

- Read Revelation 19:11–16. What parallels do you see between Habakkuk 3 and the coming of Christ in Revelation 19?

- How would you characterize Habakkuk's response in verse 16? Paraphrase your response in your own words.

- In Habakkuk's declaration of faith; how are his descriptions of difficulty especially significant in an agrarian society? What today might be parallel to the descriptions in verse 17?

- What did Habakkuk declare in verses 18–19? How did he describe God and what God did?

**S** **Seek counsel:** *What do wise people say*?

Read chapter 4 or watch a video presentation
of this chapter.  Access the QR
(Quick Response) code that
can be read by many smart
devices using a scanning app.
It allows you to immediately
watch the video. If you do not have a QR code
reader, you can access the same material at
https://vimeo.com/99048557. To the extent
you have time and ability, read the relevant
section from one of the recommended studies.
Also check out the resources available on
Bible.org.

## D Develop your response: *What do I think?*

- In essence, what is God telling us in this text? What is the main point of the passage? Write down a one-sentence statement of the main point.

- What could be "rugged terrain" for you today, perhaps something analogous to what Habakkuk describes in verse 17? In the face of your difficult circumstances, how could you rejoice in the Lord and bound like a deer?

■ Initially how do you believe the Spirit of God is moving you to respond to this passage? You will refine your response when you get to the "Move to action" section.

## ◉ Openly discuss: *What do we think?*

1. How have you identified with Habakkuk over the course of our study of this book?

2. What contrasts do you see between Habakkuk 1:1–2 and 3:1–2? How would you describe Habakkuk's transformation?

3. For what did Habakkuk ask in 3:1–2? How can we make a similar request today in light of Jesus' coming and return?

4.  As you reflect on God's coming described in 3:3–15, what images are most compelling to you? How do you feel as you read through the text?

5.  How did Habakkuk respond in 3:16? Why do you think he felt like that?

6.  Read Habakkuk's final declaration in verses 17–19. How could he rejoice in the face of the realities of verse 17? What did God do for him and for us? How can you move closer to Habakkuk's faith in the face of your struggles?

7.  How have you progressed in your understanding of God and the difficulties of this life through our study of Habakkuk? What has God taught you? What are you walking away with?

# M Move to action: *What will I do?*

In reflecting on your study of Habakkuk 3:1–19, how will you move to action? How do you believe God wants to transform you through this text?

# RECOMMENDED STUDIES

In preparing this book, I consulted the following commentaries and Bible studies on Habakkuk:

Francis I. Andersen, *Habakkuk, The Anchor Bible*, vol. 25 (New York: Doubleday, 2001).
> Advanced, technical, but the most extensive work on Habakkuk.

Ronald J. Blue, *Habakkuk, The Bible Knowledge Commentary: An Exposition of the Scriptures*, edited by J. F. Walvoord and R. B. Zuck. (Wheaton, IL: Victor Books, 1985).
> Short helpful commentary with memorable ways of communicating.

Richard D. Patterson, *Nahum, Habakkuk, Zephaniah* (Dallas: Biblical Studies Press, 2003).
> Advanced, recommended; good technical notes for advanced students and good summaries for those who like serious Bible study.

Kenneth L. Barker, *Micah, Nahum, Habakkuk, Zephaniah, The New American Commentary*, vol. 20 (Nashville: Broadman & Holman, 1999).
> Excellent evangelical commentary.

Walter Kaiser, *Micah, Nahum, Habakkuk, Zephaniah, Haggai, Zechariah, Malachi, Mastering the Old Testament*, vol. 21 (Dallas; London; Vancouver; Melbourne: Word Publishing, 1992).
>    Popular work undergirded by fine scholarship by the well-respected Walter Kaiser.

James Bruckner, *Jonah, Nahum, Habakkuk, Zephaniah: The New Application Commentary* (Grand Rapids: Zondervan, 2004).
>    Outstanding work combining up-to-date scholarship with practical application crossing the bridge well from then to now.

Mária Eszenyei Széles, *Wrath and Mercy: A Commentary on the Books of Habakkuk and Zephaniah* (Grand Rapids: Eerdmans, 1987).
>    Szeles provides penetrating theological and practical insights often missed by others.

David W. Baker, *Nahum, Habakkuk, Zephaniah: An Introduction and Commentary* (Leicester, England; Downers Grove, IL: InterVarsity Press, 1988).
>    A fine basic study.

O. Palmer Robertson, *The Books of Nahum, Habakkuk, and Zephaniah: The New International Commentary of the Old Testament* (Grand Rapids: Eerdmans, 1990).
>    Solid study.

Thomas Edward McComiskey, *The Minor Prophets: An Exegetical and Expository Commentary*, vol. 2, *Obadiah, Jonah, Micah, Nahum, and Habakkuk* (Grand Rapids: Baker Books, 1993).
> Combination of technical and advanced study with average insights.

Robert B. Chisholm Jr., *Handbook on the Prophets: Isaiah, Jeremiah, Lamentations, Ezekiel, Daniel, Minor Prophets* (Grand Rapids: Baker Academic, 2009).
> This book does an exceptionally good job of summarizing the teachings of the Old Testament prophets on a book-by-book basis while also dealing with crucial issues. Aimed at college level. Strongly recommended.

> *To the King of the ages, immortal, invisible, the only God, be honor and glory forever and ever. Amen.*
> —1 Timothy 1:17, ESV

## BRUCE B. MILLER

God has given Bruce the privilege of serving as husband to his wife, Tamara, since 1983 and father to their five children. They are also blessed with their grandchildren. God used Bruce to plant Christ Fellowship in McKinney, Texas where he currently serves as senior pastor (CFhome.org). In his spare time, he loves spending time with Tamara, playing racquetball, using a chainsaw and sitting by an open fire with his chocolate Labrador, Calvin.

His passion for leadership development led to his first book, *The Leadership Baton*, written with Jeff Jones and Rowland Forman. Bruce's heart to see people live more joyful, fulfilled lives sparked the writing of *Your Life in Rhythm*, the forerunner to *Your Church in Rhythm* which applies the concepts of rhythmic living to local churches (BruceBMiller.com).

Bruce developed the innovative six-step WISDOM Process© which serves as a learning engine in the study guides for his books *Big God in a Chaotic World—A Fresh Look at Daniel; When God Makes No Sense—A Fresh Look at Habakkuk;* and *Sexuality—Approaching Controversial Issues with Grace, Truth and Hope.*

Bruce graduated Phi Beta Kappa from the University of Texas at Austin with a B.A. in Plan II, the Honors Liberal Arts Program ('82); received a master's degree in Theology from Dallas Theological Seminary ('86); and did doctoral work at the University of Texas at Dallas in the History of Ideas (focus on philosophical hermeneutics, Hans-Georg Gadamer, and post-modernism). He taught theology for four years at Dallas Theological Seminary.

Bruce speaks and consults around the world. He founded the Centers for Church Based Training and served as Chairman of the Board for 12 years (http://ccbt.org). Bruce founded and leads Dadlin ministries, an organization committed to helping people develop wisdom for life.

You can follow Bruce on:

**Twitter** (http://twitter.com/Bruce_B_Miller)

or

**Facebook**

(https://www.facebook.com/BruceBMillerAuthor)

**Blog** (BruceBMiller.com)

To invite Bruce to speak, contact him at:

**Website** (BruceBMiller.com)

# OTHER RESOURCES

*The publishing ministry of*
*Dadlin ministries—an*
*organization committed to*
*helping people develop wisdom for life.*

**Dadlin Media**
— *wisdom for life* —

Resources by **Bruce B. Miller:**

*The Leadership Baton*
Equips you with a solution to the need
for quality leaders in local churches.
Miller provides you with a biblical
vision, a holistic approach and a
comprehensive plan.

*Your Life in Rhythm*
Offers a realistic way to overcome
our crazy, overly busy, stressed
lives. Exposes the myth of living a
"balanced" life. Miller presents
"rhythmic living" as a new
paradigm for relieving guilt and
stress, so we can accomplish more of what
matters most in life—with more freedom, peace,
fulfillment and hope.

*Your Church in Rhythm*
Most pastors try to do everything at once, and they feel guilty if even one aspect of their church ministry is neglected in the process. Instead, Miller proposes replacing this exhausting notion of "balance" with the true-to-life concept of "rhythm." Churches, just like people, should focus on the seasons and the cycles of ministry programs. That way, leaders can avoid burnout by focusing only on each issue at the time that it matters most.

*Big God in a Chaotic World—A Fresh Look at Daniel*
Shows we can live faithfully in this sinful, out-of-control world when we get a fresh vision of our big God. Daniel opens our eyes to see the God who is bigger than the problems in

our world, bigger than all our fears, fires and lions.

*Same-Sex Marriage—A Bold Call to the Church in Response to the Supreme Court's Decision*

In response to this cultural crisis, the church should step up with a Christlike response that stuns the world, and draws people to Jesus Christ with counter-cultural love.

*Sexuality—Approaching
Controversial Issues with Grace,
Truth and Hope*
Addresses the purposes of sex in
marriage, singleness,
cohabitation, homosexuality
(and more), with fresh biblical
insights filled with grace.

**Coming Soon:**
*Never the Same—A Fresh Look at
the Sermon on the Mount*

*Miracles—A Fresh Look at Jesus*

For more information on current and upcoming
books, go to **BruceBMiller.com**.

McKinney, TX  75070

# FROM THE AUTHOR

Thank you for taking time to read this book. My hope is that you have found wisdom for your life. I love hearing from my readers. Feel free to contact me if you have any questions or thoughts you'd like to share. Email me at author@brucebmiller.com.

If you enjoyed this book, there are several things you can do to help others:

- Consider leaving a review on Amazon and on Goodreads, or your favorite online retailer. Honest reader reviews help others decide whether they'll enjoy a book.

- You can lend this book to a friend who might enjoy it.

- Check my website (BruceBmiller.com) or Facebook page (BruceBMillerAuthor) to find my other books and new releases. You can sign up for my newsletter to receive the latest news.

Sincerely,

*Bruce*

1. Ronald J. Blue, *Habakkuk, The Bible Knowledge Commentary: An Exposition of the Scriptures*, edited by J. F. Walvoord and R. B. Zuck (Wheaton, IL: Victor Books, 1985).

2. Walter Kaiser, *Mastering the Old Testament*, Vol. 21: *Micah, Nahum, Habakkuk, Zephaniah, Haggai, Zechariah, Malachi* (Dallas; London; Vancouver; Melbourne: Word Publishing, 1992), 153.

3. O. Palmer Robertson, *The Books of Nahum, Habakkuk, and Zephaniah: The New International Commentary of the Old Testament* (Grand Rapids: Eerdmans, 1990), 152.

4. James Bruckner, *Jonah, Nahum, Habakkuk, Zephaniah: The New Application Commentary* (Grand Rapids: Zondervan, 2004), 221.

5. Bruckner, *Jonah, Nahum, Habakkuk, Zephaniah*, 218.

6. Robertson, *The Books of Nahum, Habakkuk, and Zephaniah*, 162.

7. Kaiser, *Mastering the Old Testament,* 162.

8. Richard Whitaker et al., *The Abridged Brown-Driver-Briggs Hebrew-English Lexicon of the Old Testament: From A Hebrew and English Lexicon of the Old Testament* by Francis Brown, S.R. Driver

and Charles Briggs, Based on the *Lexicon of Wilhelm Gesenius* (Boston; New York: Houghton, Mifflin, 1906), Reference BDB 53.1 Logos.

9. Bruckner, *Jonah, Nahum, Habakkuk, Zephaniah*, 236.

10. Robert B. Chisholm Jr., *Handbook on the Prophets: Isaiah, Jeremiah, Lamentations, Ezekiel, Daniel, Minor Prophets* (Grand Rapids: Baker Academic, 2009), 438.

11. Bruckner, *Jonah, Nahum, Habakkuk, Zephaniah*, 236.

12. Bruckner, *Jonah, Nahum, Habakkuk, Zephaniah*, 240.

13. Chisholm, *Handbook on the Prophets,* 438.

14. Mária Eszenyei Széles, *Wrath and Mercy: A Commentary on the Books of Habakkuk and Zephaniah* (Grand Rapids: Eerdmans, 1987), 35.

15. Bruckner, *Jonah, Nahum, Habakkuk, Zephaniah*, 233–234.

Made in the USA
Middletown, DE
04 August 2021